A Cornishman Cruises the Western Mediterranean

George Williams

Copyright © 2015 George Williams

All rights reserved.

ISBN-13: 978-1507561768

CONTENTS

INTRODUCTION..7

THE ALLURE OF THE MEDITERRANEAN................................10

FLY CRUISES, OR SAILING TO AND FROM THE UK?...............14

PORTS WHERE YOU CAN START AND END YOUR CRUISES...19

SAIL-AWAY..21

GIBRALTAR - GATEWAY TO THE MEDITERRANEAN..............24

SPAIN...39

ORGANISED TOURS, OR PLAN YOUR OWN VISITS?.............80

FRANCE..86

ITALY..104

NORTH AFRICA – MOROCCO..178

TIME TO GO HOME..181

ABOUT THE AUTHOR...184

OTHER BOOKS BY THIS AUTHOR.......................................185

A Cornishman Cruises the Western Mediterranean

Introduction

Yes I am a Cornishman and very proud of it. I grew up and lived there for nearly forty years with the sea virtually in my backyard, but in all that time my experiences of going to sea were limited to a handful of ferry crossings to the Isle of Wight, France and Belgium. To be honest, those trips were the limit of any holiday that me and my family had as I am terrified of flying, and I have long since given up any attempt to overcome those fears. My wife (Deb) was very patient about my phobia but at least she managed to take our two children away for a holiday by plane. Little did she know just how frightened I was for them while they were away, always fearing that I would never see them again.

It was only in the year 2000 that a truly special holiday was considered, as it was our 25th and Silver Wedding Anniversary. There were moments when beads of sweat broke out on my forehead as I thought that air travel would be necessary, but relief came when we looked up to the top shelf in a travel agency and saw a brochure for P&O Cruises.

After much deliberation we chose a cruise that took us from Southampton all the way to Istanbul, with a superb variety of other ports on the outward and return journey. Almost instantly we came under the spell of cruising and there was no going back...we were hooked!

Fourteen years on and we have cruised at least once every year and sometimes more often. We have been on twenty cruises so far, all with P&O, and have even sailed completely around the world on a three-month adventure in 2012.

Yes I called it an adventure. In fact every cruise has been more than a holiday, because if you have a fear of flying then going abroad becomes almost unthinkable so to have been able to view so much has been something I never expected.

The experiences were so memorable that I started to write books about our holidays. I had spent the second half of my career producing technical engineering training material, and being able to write about my own thoughts was so much more fulfilling. Of course it took a long time, and in fact the first book (A Cornishman Goes Cruising) took ten years to complete. I eventually self-published it just in time for our world circumnavigation, and it was perhaps pushing the fantasy a bit, but when people asked what I did I responded with **"I write books"**.

There is a book dedicated to that world cruise (Around the World Without Wings), and another about our various visits to Venice, but this particular one is to give readers a chance to share my thoughts on the many adventures to the Western Mediterranean. My recollections are based on fourteen years of cruises on different ships, with some of the cities and islands being just one-off visits, but other places have been enjoyed on several occasions.

So sit back, relax, and I hope you will soon get an idea of just how enjoyable it has been as this Cornishman cruised around the western Mediterranean.

The Allure of the Mediterranean

The name Mediterranean can be split into *'Med'* meaning middle, and *'Terran'* meaning earth or land. Hence we have '**In the Middle of Land'**. The Mediterranean Sea is a virtually enclosed area of water, apart from the gateway to the Atlantic Ocean in the west at the Straits of Gibraltar. In the east it is linked to the Dardanelles giving access to Sea of Marmara, and further still to the Black Sea via the Bosporus. In the south-east there is access to the Suez Canal, which makes the Mediterranean Sea a seriously shorter route to the East than sailing around the African continent.

Three continents border it, with Europe to the north, Africa to the south and Asia to the east. It has an area of approximately 1,000,000 square miles (2,500,000 square kilometres) and is split into two basins (west and east). As a rough guide, the western basin is from the Straits of Gibraltar to the Straits of Messina at the north of the Island of Sicily. In general terms the Mediterranean is a single area of water, but within it there are other named seas with the Aegean to the east of Greece, the Ionian between Sicily and Greece, the Adriatic to the north-east of Italy, and the lesser-known Tyrrhenian between the western Italian coast and the Island of Sardinia.

Ignoring ongoing political changes in national identities, here is a list of the countries bordering the

Mediterranean. Starting at the west and travelling east we have Spain, France, Italy, Slovenia, Croatia, perhaps a tiny bit of Bosnia and Herzegovina, certainly Montenegro, Albania, Greece, and Turkey with its European and Asian areas. Continuing south there is Syria, Lebanon, Israel, but sadly nowhere called Palestine. Returning along the southern coast there is Egypt, Libya, Tunisia, Algeria and finally Morocco. There are also the islands of Malta and Cyprus with their own identities, and really stretching the point even further there is even a little bit of Britain at Gibraltar.

The weather is a mix of temperate warm winters and hot dry summers. The sea is clear, and with blue skies above it seems to be just so much more colourful than around our own shores. To put it mildly it is the sort of place most British people adore either as a summer pilgrimage to the hot sunshine or as a winter getaway from our drab, cold, or wet months.

For most of the thousands of holidaymakers who take a week or more in the sunshine of Barcelona, Malaga, Nice, or Cannes the Mediterranean is simply the view from their golden beaches. Others delight in the history of Florence and Naples, or the pleasures of unique cities like Venice and Dubrovnik. If mainland venues are not your thing then the islands of Sardinia, Corsica, Sicily, Malta, Cyprus, the magical Greek Islands, the Balearics and the stunningly beautiful Capri offer a different escape from the humdrum world of work. Then of course there is perhaps more mystery and intrigue to be found in the hot countries of the African coast.

Getting there is a short plane trip. From London to western cities in Spain and France it should take less than two hours, and Italian destinations are between two and three hours. A Turkish resort would be four hours and African destinations would be three to four hours.

Alternatively if you want to sample a selection of what is on offer, there are hundreds of cruises sailing from a vast number of Mediterranean ports. Or if you are a non-flyer (like myself) you can hop on a ship at Southampton and less than three days later turn left towards Gibraltar and enjoy being pampered as you visit several of the most beautiful cities and islands on offer, while soaking up the sunshine on a floating hotel without the stress at airports and flight delays.

On a cruise the Mediterranean is no longer just a view from a beach or a hotel, it is the back garden that greets you each morning when you wake up. It is a pathway taking you between holiday destinations but at a more sedate pace of travel. On most nights your floating hotel takes you from one location to another with no need to pack and unpack. Entertainment will keep you occupied each evening after you have sampled a superb dinner. Yes there will be the occasional day at sea for the longer parts of the cruise, but these days are your chance to relax, unwind from whatever has stressed you, lay in the sun, read that book you just couldn't find the time for at home, or maybe learn to dance or listen to a talk from a celebrity.

Welcome to my world.

Deb and I have sailed around the Mediterranean on numerous occasions and I have already talked about trips to the Eastern Basin in an earlier book (A Cornishman cruises to Venice), so in this one I am going to concentrate on our experiences in the west. Some of the places we've docked at just once, while others have become regular stops, and though familiar, they never cease to thrill us with their architecture, culture, and friendly people...

...oh and the almost guaranteed warmth.

Fly Cruises, or sailing to and from the UK?

There are four ways of going on a cruise holiday.

1. A fly-cruise is probably the most popular method, where you fly to one of the many ports around the world where cruise ships start and finish their trips. For Mediterranean holidays there are several places to embark on a cruise, and there is a wide choice of cruise company, as well as size and style of ship.
2. For the non-flying community, like me, the favoured option is to start and finish our holidays at a UK port. Personally, we favour Southampton but there are several other places around the country. The non-fly option may restrict the choice of cruise a little, but if you find something that works for you, why take a chance on something else?
3. You can attempt to be a stowaway. I am sure some have got away with it but modern-day security is very comprehensive and so this is probably not a viable solution.
4. You could become a member of the crew, either as a merchant seaman or perhaps as one of the entertainment staff?
   You are then paid to sail around the world and some of that time must be like being on holiday. The drawback with this idea is that when you have

worked for several years on a ship it might become just another job.

…work experience sounds a good idea though.

So probably discounting options 3 and 4, let's consider the other types of cruising and I will try and give an unbiased view of their positives and negatives.

+++

Fly-Cruises

The obvious advantage for most people is that a three-hour flight will bring you to your ship that is already sitting in a Mediterranean port with the sunshine and warmth you crave. This means a seven day (or longer) holiday starts just a few hours after leaving home.

There is a wide choice of shipping lines and types of ship for fly-cruises. Almost every company, from budget lines through to the top-end six-star luxury ones, have home ports around the Mediterranean with well-practiced slick passenger transfers from airports. This allows a holidaymaker to be worshipping the sun by early afternoon on a ship that satisfies their bank balance, and their desired levels of comfort and facilities.

Fly-cruises also allow those with less than jolly-jack-tar stomachs to avoid a couple of days at either end of the cruise in the choppier – and sometimes uncomfortably rough – waters of the English Channel, and especially the dreaded Bay of Biscay.

Cruise companies vary their itineraries, so during a typical week (or fortnight) at sea the holiday will include places you might have visited before and others that are new.

You might want to have a *Cruise and Stay* option where the holiday includes a few days in a hotel at the beginning or end of the cruise. This can be a wonderful way of exploring a city at leisure, something not always possible during a stop on a cruise.

The fly-cruise experience can be *full-on* from the first evening to the last morning. Partying often starts as the ship leaves port just a couple of hours after you board, and by the next morning, while your hangover is still fresh, the ship has arrived at its first destination. You can get off to have a tour, perhaps just go for a walk and a spot of shopping, or maybe relax on a beach until the head clears and you are ready for the evening party to continue.

On the negative side, that *full-on* experience may not be to your liking.

It can mean that there are fewer sea days, when the ship is sailing during the daytime hours. Many cruise fanatics actually like sea days. Life on board is a little slower allowing you to experience more of what the ship can offer. You can also become a little in tune with nature, as the sea rushes by and the breeze ruffles your hair.

When a ship sails from a port in Spain, France, or Italy the likelihood is that there will be a mixture of nationalities and thus a variety of languages being used by passengers and crew. This can be seen positively as a cultural experience but conversely you might be uncomfortable, especially as you wait for an announcement to be made in a language you recognise.

Sailing to and from UK

This is the obvious solution for those who dislike or have a phobia about flying.

With no air travel restrictions there are no weight limits for baggage, so a greater choice of clothes can be taken. The only limit on luggage is how much you can fit into your car!

Although there may be some passengers who have flown in from other parts of the world to join the ship, it will be generally a British cruise with a familiar culture and English being the only language spoken.

You will have a greater chance of experiencing real sailing, with a couple of days at the beginning and end of the cruise to get between home waters and the

Mediterranean. I rather enjoy sea days as they allow me to slowly switch off thoughts of home and work, before turning left at Trafalgar Point and truly beginning the holiday. Before I retired I used the return trip up the English Channel to reflect on the holiday and get my head back in gear ready to go to work again.

Sea days also give more opportunities to sample the daytime activities on board the ship. The talks by professional speakers or celebrities may appeal, or perhaps you may want to join in with people who are learning to dance or play Bridge. Many people just stroll around the decks and look for passing ships and occasional dolphins. There is time to read a book while lying on a lounger until it gets too hot and you need to cool down in one of the swimming pools.

Yes, of course the journey to the Mediterranean can be rough and people do suffer from sea sickness. It is an awful experience and many simply take their remedy and curl up in their cabins for two days until the sea calms down. I usually have moments on a cruise where my head and stomach moan, but taking a little white pill as soon as the feelings start usually deals with my problems. In fourteen years I have only been sick on two occasions, and they were when I ignored my symptoms for too long.

Ports where you can start and end your cruises

No-Fly Cruises

Humour me initially as I talk about the options for embarking and disembarking your holiday ships at a British port.

Without a doubt Southampton is the biggest and busiest cruise ship port in the UK, with four dedicated terminals for the industry and a fifth planned. The Mayflower Terminal was where our first maritime adventure started and is the home of P&O ships. Cunard have their nominated terminal called, appropriately enough, the QE2 Terminal. However, the terminals are only nominally allocated to these two shipping lines, as all four terminals are available to all ships from all lines. This has to be the case in today's holiday business, as there are often four cruise ships in port at the same time. There is also the City Cruise Terminal and the Ocean Cruise Terminal and the fifth terminal was due to have opened in 2013 so I assume it must be nearing completion.

As well as the P&O and Cunard lines, Southampton also has regular arrivals and departures from other companies such as Princess Cruises, Fred Olsen, Saga, Royal Caribbean, Celebrity and MSC (Mediterranean Shipping Company).

Around the coast of Britain you could also join a ship at Dover, Harwich, Belfast, Tilbury, Hull, Newcastle, Edinburgh, Leith, Greenock, and Plymouth, and many others besides.

Although the size of their ships is a limiting factor for some ports, the following cruise lines could also popup anywhere around the country: Disney ships, Hebridean Cruises, NCL, Swan Hellenic, Holland America, Seabourn, Crystal Cruises, Silversea, plus many other smaller individual ships.

Fly-Cruise Ports

For those who prefer fly-cruises, the Mediterranean options are too many to name, but the main ones are:

Spain – Barcelona, Palma, Cadiz, Malaga, Valencia...probably others

France – Nice, Marseille, Cannes, Cherbourg

Italy – Genoa, Venice, Rome (Civitavecchia), Florence, Naples

These are the major ports that offer cruise departures but there are many other options besides these.

Sail-away

Leaving Southampton at the beginning of another cruise is always a moment that makes the back of my neck tingle, and my mind races in anticipation of what is to come. Even after fourteen years and more than twenty sail-aways, I still adore the moment. Perhaps its impact on me has decreased over the years because of cost cutting and environmental pressures, but it never ceases to have hundreds of passengers leaning over the open-deck rails or looking down from their cabin balconies as the ropes are dropped into the Solent, ship's horn blasts a farewell, and a watery gap appears between dockside and the hull.

In this book I will gloss over too much detail of our very first cruise in 2000, as the only western Mediterranean port we called at was a half day in Gibraltar, but I do remember vividly that first day on board the beautiful ship *Oriana*. The complete 17-day cruise was a magical experience from our planning and preparing over several months, to the moment we saw the funnel for the very first time and gasped in amazement, right the way to the excitement hangover that hit me when we arrived back home.

I can almost hear the words of our first ever sail-away as Captain Richard Fenelowe announced that ***"...all our pre-departure checks have been completed and we are***

ready to proceed to sea". There was a band playing patriotic tunes, and as the ship's horn sounded they were already playing Land of Hope and Glory and the conductor was enthusiastically waving a large union flag. We were sipping a glass of champagne looking down to the dockside where shore-side workers were looking up at us: some waved a goodbye, signalling it was time for them to go home for dinner.

As water appeared below confirming we were on our way, everyone flung their rolls of paper streamers in unison from each deck making a spider's web of tangling coloured paper that fluttered down into the water. Hundreds of us waved and cheered at friends and families who in those days could watch from the viewing enclosure of the Mayflower Terminal.

Within a few minutes the shouts from shore could no longer be heard and the excitement on the ship calmed as passengers returned to their cabins to unpack their luggage or began to explore their temporary home until it was time for our dinner.

Nowadays the excitement still exists, especially with newer cruisers, but the atmosphere has changed. A band does sometimes appear for the start of a world cruise, or a maiden voyage perhaps, but paper streamers are gone because of the risk to the environment of waste paper in our already contaminated waters. Generally the sail-away party is now on the ship where there is always a place for the passengers to gather near a bar and dance around the pool. Sometimes the resident band will play live, but just as often it is the ship's DJ playing the usual party songs while waiters sell champagne, or more likely pints of Stella and glasses of white wine. Flags are handed out to be waved as the photographers snap hundreds of exorbitantly priced memories in the hope of tempting a few of us to buy one.

Fewer people stare over the side of the ship anymore. The cruise experience is being targeted at a different audience of younger families who want that party experience from beginning to end of their holiday. Some experienced cruise passengers have suggested that many of the cruise lines are trying to recreate a Holiday Camp culture, and maybe in order for the industry to survive and flourish it is possibly the only way forward. But thankfully for the thousands of longer-in-the-tooth passengers like ourselves, there are still some traditional ships that cater for the older, but still young at heart, passengers who continue to crave patriotic bands, streamers, and watching from the promenade deck rails.

Gibraltar - Gateway to the Mediterranean

It is time now to look at some of the experiences that we have had over the years.

The first cruise that took us around the ports of the Western Mediterranean was for 14 days at the end of July 2001 aboard a ship called *Arcadia*. Some of you will have already looked at the ship's name and year with confusion in your mind. Presently P&O has a ship called *Arcadia* in its fleet but the one I am talking about was an earlier vessel that spent a short time with the fleet before becoming *Ocean Village* sailing out of Australia and is now called the *Pacific Pearl*.

By today's standards she is small, with just over 63,000 tonnes capable of carrying 1800 passengers. Back in 2001 Arcadia was considered large, and she towered over the vast majority of other cruise ships. She was always called a friendly ship and had vast areas of open deck for people to lie in the sun, or play in the pools.

As this was our second cruise we felt we were now seasoned cruisers, and were able to bore newcomers with our stories as well as occasionally giving some reasonable advice. Our voyage down the Channel wasn't rough and I have video footage of waves and swell of less than a metre as we crossed the Bay of Biscay.

The weather was typically British as we left Southampton, meaning we wore jumpers, but by the second day Deb was sunbathing on Promenade Deck as the sun warmed up. We regularly used the swimming pools and dried off on the recliners that surrounded them. *Arcadia* even had a pool where you could sit at stools that surrounded a bar that was actually in the water.

On Day Three we woke up and quickly realised we were sailing more to the east than south and the morning announcement from the Bridge confirmed our arrival at Gibraltar was not too far away.

We were sailing through the Straits of Gibraltar where the Atlantic Ocean becomes the Mediterranean Sea. The Straits is the gap of water that separates the continents of Europe and Africa. At its narrowest point it is around nine miles wide and it becomes a bottle-neck for a very busy shipping lane that has vessels of all sizes coming and going from the Far East to and from northern Europe. It is one of the many areas of the world where the sea becomes what is known as a *Traffic Separation Scheme,* which is a little like a dual carriageway system, but without any physical barriers. The rules are that ships must sail on the right-hand side, so coming into the Mediterranean they sail on the African side and when leaving they sail closer to the European coast.

That is all very well until you consider the extra problems of sea traffic crossing between the North African coast to Southern Europe, and ships like us turning into Gibraltar. So there are shipping lanes without barriers and junction points where ships can cross. All shipping movements are controlled by the International Maritime Organisations, but areas of water like this require ships' captains to be extra careful.

On this cruise Captain Hamish Reid successfully got us through this tricky bit of water and very soon the familiar shape of the Rock of Gibraltar came into view.

Going back to the times of myths and legends, the Rock of Gibraltar was seen as the northerly promontory guarding the European side of the Straits, and is historically referred to as one of the *'Pillars of Hercules'*. Although the actual site is disputed, there is a southern promontory on the African Coast making up this ancient historical pairing. The significance of the *'Pillars of Hercules'* is that it refers to a location said to be the furthest westerly point that Hercules travelled to while performing his twelve labours.

The politically sensitive British Oversea Protectorate of Gibraltar sits at the end of the Iberian Peninsula and is a small patch of land of less than three square miles. Looking at it on a map, it is an arrow shaped lump pointing southwards from a narrow isthmus of Southern Spain. Most of this lump of Britain is made up of the

426-metre high Rock of Gibraltar that towers over its city that has some 30,000 inhabitants squeezed into it. The Rock runs north to south and leaves just a narrow strip of land around it with beaches on the east and south. The largest populated area is on the western side, and includes the harbour and yacht marinas. To the north is the airport with its runway which starts out in the bay and runs all the way from west to east. The road between Gibraltar and Spain actually crosses the runway with a border checkpoint on the northern side controlling the flow of traffic and people in an out of this contested little piece of Britain.

Sailing into Gibraltar is quite spectacular and many sailors express a thrill as they arrive. After two days at sea most passengers were looking forward to getting their feet back on dry and steady land again.

At the harbour there is space for a single large cruise ship, although there are other berths where a smaller vessel can dock at the same time. On one of our other visits to Gibraltar we had a planned lunchtime arrival but were delayed for thirty minutes while we waited for the QE2 to depart the berth. This was during the final year of this magnificent ship's life at sea, and as she was being guided out by two tugs the passengers waved between the two ships as horns blasted out across the water. It was worth the delay to experience such a special sight.

Between the two docking berths there is a small terminal where the passengers walk through to North Mole Road which leads into the town. Although most people walk to the town, there are always numerous taxis (small minibuses) doing their best to attract fares. They are not expensive and save the passengers walking the straight mile or so of road that is exposed to the hot sunshine. At the far end of North Mole Road you pass the first of the shops and businesses before coming to a roundabout where most people get out of their taxis to walk under the old Garrison Wall through the Casemates Gate into the large square of the same name.

Casemates Square is surrounded by cafes, bars, market stalls, souvenir shops and artisan studios. It is where cruise ship passengers can have a little taste of Britain with a plate of fish and chips and a pint of beer but most visitors simply have a quick look around before crossing the square and arriving at the westerly end of Main Street. This shopping street runs virtually all the way to the eastern end of the town where there is another Gate under a further section of the Garrison Wall. Main Street is narrow, and each time we have visited there it has been packed with tourists shopping for souvenirs and locals buying their daily needs.

I have written a lot about Gibraltar in my other books but the essence of my thoughts are that even if it is a British Protectorate, the folk of Britain have unusually protective feelings towards it. It is a lump of rock at the southern tip of Spain that was captured by Anglo-Dutch forces in 1704 during the Spanish War of Succession. In 1713 the Dutch ceded it in perpetuity to Britain under the Treaty of Utrecht. It was an important naval base for hundreds of years and Britain maintained a garrison there until quite recently.

There are still examples that keep it looking like *home* with colonial-style buildings, and red post boxes. The police wear the same familiar sort of hats, and the accepted language is English. My issue is that most of the population are several generations on from pure British stock: they look remarkably Hispanic and talk with Spanish accents. A high percentage of the shops are owned by Asian families, but the major shopping attraction with visitors remains the lure of cheap tax-free items. Although bargains can be found, much of what is on offer can be bought just as cheap on the internet.

In its favour is the wonderful climate and friendly people that makes it quite a superb place to come for a holiday. A real home-from-home improved by the warmth and sunshine we crave for.

+++

Let me return to our visit on 24th July 2001.

Over the years we have been careful not to waste too much money on P&O organised tours unless it is the first time we have visited a particular port. We had been to

Gibraltar for a half-day stop the previous year but only went for a walk to the town and window-shopped in Main Street. This time we had booked on to a tour that gave us a glimpse of several parts of the Rock.

One thing to remember is that Gibraltar is a small place with narrow roads but a lot of traffic. They don't have the usual large coaches, and tourists are driven around in mini-buses that double up as taxis. Our driver was a friendly and knowledgeable local with a dusky complexion and a Spanish accent. After fighting our way from the dock to the main roads he took us to Europa Point, the southerly tip of Gibraltar from where we could look up at the towering Rock. We stopped very close to the stunningly beautiful Ibrahim-al-Ibrahim Mosque, and also had a view out to sea past the Europa Point Lighthouse.

Although it was misty when we docked, the sun had come out and it was wonderfully warm. Our cameras were going frantic capturing memories of the iconic Rock as well as the white mosque and the lighthouse with ships in the distance in the Mediterranean Sea.

Our tour only allowed a brief time at each location, so we were quickly back on the rather hot mini-bus and making our way back towards the town before turning upwards and our next stop at St Michael's Cave.

There are a number of natural caves and tunnels under the Rock, but many more were man-made for wartime use. St Michael's Cave is a natural one some 300-metres up from sea level. The Rock is limestone, with caves created where water soaks into the ground and forms an acid that erodes the rock away. Acid continues to drip slowly from above making icicle-shaped stalactites which appear to hang from the ceiling: drips falling from them reach the floor and form stalagmites which look like icicle shapes pointing upwards.

Left undisturbed for hundreds of thousands of years the scene created is stunningly magical and St Michael's Cave is probably one of the most beautiful anywhere. It is a series of caverns with huge open areas that have been illuminated with coloured lights to turn the spectacle into a fairy grotto. One of the larger caverns is used for concerts, and has a stage area and seating for hundreds to enjoy the music. Every time you look upwards the sheer numbers of eerie stalactites clumped together create a scene looking as if the roof had been made of wax which had been heated up until it melted to form this beautiful, but sometimes grotesque sculpture. These caves really are well worth a visit.

Suitable impressed by the beauty created by nature, we came out into the natural light again and made the short drive to where some of the Rock's colony of, Barbary Macaque monkeys could be seen. As he tempted the animals closer with a pocket full of peanuts, our driver warned us to guard our possessions from the curious creatures that imagined everything we were carrying was a possible meal or a glittering prize. Handbags are often snatched from shoulders, and wallets from pockets of any unsuspecting visitor, and the macaques quickly scamper away over the railing and into the woods with their treasures.

...Oh well, yet another insurance claim to be made!

That was the tour completed, and we drove back down the hill to the town area. Some of the passengers were taken to the dockside while others like us stayed in the shopping area to look around for a little while longer.

Our travels have resulted in small souvenirs from all over the world and this was a chance to find something from Gibraltar. To our sadness there was little here that wasn't imported and much fell very disappointingly into the category of *Tat*. At least there was a chance to enjoy an ice-cream, and we did buy some lace items to take home. It was on this visit that I even bought a digital video camera that recorded our cruise moments for several years to come.

That was almost it for that visit, with just the mile stroll from Casemates Square at the end of Main Street back along the dock road to where our air-conditioned ship brought relief from the blazing sun.

+++

Next year on 21st August 2002, we were back in Gibraltar on board Oriana. This time we had another organised tour to keep us amused during the morning.

It was a wonderful experience with a couple of hours on a small pleasure craft called the *Brixham Belle* looking for dolphins in Gibraltar Bay. I somehow recollect seeing this boat in South Devon many years before when we had numerous holidays around that area, but now we were on-board her looking for these amazing creatures.

As well as being a beautiful warm and sunny morning, the dolphins were in a good mood. They came up close to the little boat, making a group of British tourists very happy. It was only a small group (or pod) of dolphins, but they came so close that we could almost touch them over the side of the craft. They swam and rolled in the water, sometimes showing their athleticism by jumping up, effortlessly arching their bodies, and then diving back into their watery habitat with hardly a splash.

While those with still cameras struggled to spot and capture images of the dolphins I quietly left my video camera recording as I looked around. When I returned home and looked at the footage, there were many minutes of the water but there were also a few sensational seconds of the dolphins at play.

After a delightful morning there was still time after lunch to walk into the town and look around the shops again before returning to Oriana and sailing on into the Mediterranean.

+++

In 2010 while on the homeward journey on the present Arcadia we had another organised tour that took us to look at the caves and tunnels used during the Second World War under the Rock itself. There are miles of tunnels that were made to allow movement from one area to another, but many caves were either dug out or extended to become storage points for food or ammunition. The tunnels had miles of pipework and cabling for light and power, as well as vast sections of shelving and other caged areas where a greater level of security was necessary. There was even a hospital, completely hidden and protected from aerial or naval attacks. Wards, beds and examples of surgical equipment still remain, giving the visitor an idea of the serious operational importance of these caves.

Most of the tunnels were huge, with smooth floors giving no difficulty standing up straight as we walked along, but others were less comfortable. They were steep and lower, making it easy to slip or bang heads as we struggled along, but the secrets revealed were worth the effort. The soldiers had mapped and named the tunnels and many signs still exist either as wooden boards with printed names, or just simple painted markers on the walls. Lots of messages had been etched onto the walls for posterity, with names of soldiers and dates of their adventures.

I was amazed by the scale of the excavation and construction that had been done, which was really a small town camouflaged by the Rock itself.

After half an hour wandering around the tunnels and caves we had lost all sense of direction. As the guide led us down to the end of another tunnel there was a sensational surprise as he took us in small groups onto an observation opening looking down several hundreds of feet at the view below. I think everyone initially gasped.

This particular observation point looked northwards, with stunning views over some of the busy town, but the view was dominated by the airport and Spain beyond it. The vast runway stretched from left to right and was being crossed by streams of cars and pedestrians going to and from the frontier checkpoint. Unfortunately we were not treated to an airplane arrival or departure when the runway would have to be cleared. We were shown building work that would soon be completed to provide a new terminal building for the airport, and saw planes waiting on the tarmac to load holidaymakers before taking them home.

Looking in a slightly different direction we spotted the cemetery, and from our height the graves were visible just as rows of tiny rectangles. The guide pointed out that the majority of the graves faced in the same direction, but a few were at a different angle, indicating alternative religious faiths share this resting place.

After a terrific time inside the Rock we were finally returned to the outside world with a few minutes to look at some gun emplacements before ending our tour with a quick visit to see the macaques playing in the sunshine.

+++

We have not had any other organised tours while in Gibraltar, but we have wandered along Main Street looking at the shops on all of our visits, and sometimes explored a little beyond the shops. Our greatest discovery was when our original plan was to go up the Rock on the cable car, but my fear of heights got the better of me. Fortunately near to the cable car station we saw a sign for the Trafalgar Cemetery that attracted our attention.

The small cemetery is in a little glade just on the other side of the gateway at the eastern end of Main Street. It is so peaceful here, apart from the birds saying hello and welcoming us to their homes. The graves date back to the years following the Battle of Trafalgar that took place in October 1805. Many of the gravestones tell short stories of their occupants, some are of officers while others simple seamen who died miles from home. That half an hour was a quiet moment just walking up and down looking at inscriptions and headstone artwork. We enjoyed it so much that we went back again on another visit to the Rock. It somehow feels more memorable than looking at shop after shop selling bottles of whisky or laptops and cameras.

Don't be afraid to leave the crowds of Main Street and investigate the narrow roads that lead off it. There is at least one museum that we found where you can browse the history of the place and its people.

We have never had fish and chips or a glass of beer, but we do always savour an ice-cream as we watch the crowds of bargain hunters. If our stop here is at the beginning of a cruise we will usually buy a bottle of cola and a few crisps or some chocolate for those odd moments on the ship when a cold drink and simple snack tempts us in the cabin.

At the end of any cruise ship visit, the harbour road is packed with passengers returning with carrier bags, holdalls or even wheeled suitcases full of treats for the dedicated bargain hunters. The sunshine and heat take their toll of those who drank too much, especially as there is no public toilet on that road for relief. Back on board the ship there are two possible emotions. If Gibraltar was the first stop on a cruise then everyone is looking forward to the sunshine of the Mediterranean, whilst if it is the final stop then passengers have just a couple of days left before arriving back in Britain with their holiday over.

I may not share the same patriotic fervour that many British visitors express for Gibraltar, but our visits have always been enjoyable and there is always something to look at or do to occupy the hours in this quirky little bit of Britain.

+++

Anyway, back in July 2001, Captain Reid welcomed us all back on board our temporary home and he announced our departure from Gibraltar to start our crossing of the Mediterranean Sea towards our next port. We sailed south until far enough off the coast and then *Arcadia* turned to the east. I always give a little sigh of pleasure at this point of a cruise knowing that unless we are very unlucky, the sea will be calm, the sun will be shining, and the temperatures will be high for the next few days.

Spain

Having dealt with the tiny bit of Britain sitting in the Mediterranean I will take you to the other countries we have visited in this beautiful sea. The first one on my list is Spain. Gibraltar is just a small pimple attached to this country that has so much to offer a visitor.

We have been to various Spanish ports on various ships so the following pages deal with over ten years of cruising adventures. To make geographical sense I will work my way from west to east along a coastline famous for holiday dreams.

Cadiz

Perhaps I shouldn't include Cadiz in the ports of the Western Mediterranean. I have my doubts if it is actually in the Mediterranean as it is a little too far to the west and hence more in the Atlantic Ocean. Nevertheless, I am putting it into the list of Spanish ports because it is so often a calling place just before, or just after passing through the Straits of Gibraltar.

Wherever it actually is, we have been to Cadiz on five cruises and it is one of our most visited ports during the last 14 years.

Within the region of Andalusia, Cadiz is a province in south western Spain and its capital is the city of the same name. It was founded as a trading post (with the name Gadir) by the Phoenicians in 1100 BC.

For the confused (like me) the Phoenicians came from a country somewhere in the area that we know today as Lebanon.

Anyway, over the centuries Cadiz changed hands several times, with the Carthaginians controlling it before the Romans came along...as they did seemingly everywhere. After that the Moors had a spell in charge during the first century AD, and they stayed put until Alphonso X of Castile defeated them in 1262. Cadiz then made a bit of a name for itself as the place where Christopher Columbus (and others) set sail to find the rest of the world.

In 1587 a certain Francis Drake caused mayhem by attacking the city and sinking several ships while he hung around there for three days. The ships involved were a part of the Spanish Armada and Drake's little adventure went down in British history as the *'Singeing of the King of Spain's Beard'*. Cadiz continued to be a popular place to attack over the following centuries but things seem to have quietened down now.

The city stands on a spit of land that sticks out into the Atlantic Ocean and is about 50 miles from the entry to the Mediterranean. This makes it unusual as it is almost completely surrounded by water. It has a population of around 130,000 and with its long and chequered history has examples of many different styles of architecture. To put it simply, Cadiz is a beautiful city.

We arrived there for the first time in July 2004 on the wonderful ship *Oriana,* spending a day there on our way down to the Canaries. Our next visits were in 2007 and 2010, both times on *Arcadia*, and the following year we were back again, this time on *Aurora*. Our latest visit was in June 2013 on board *Arcadia* again.

+++

Cadiz is perfect for cruise ship passengers. The port is large, and on a busy day there can be four or five ships in dock sending thousands of eager holidaymakers in search of something to look at and something to buy. A local complimentary shuttle bus takes passengers from any ship to the dock gates where it is so easy to get into the bustling city. At the dock gates there are nearly always hop-on-hop-off buses waiting, but we usually walk across the road and go into a park called the Plaza de Espana. This park is dominated by a monument that celebrates the introduction of the country's constitution in 1812. It is a large structure with lots to see and photograph, and in front of it is an eternal flame to remember the dead through the wars.

In the park there are plenty of places to sit and look at the trees and listen to the birds before moving on into the backstreets of Cadiz. You don't have to walk far before squares appear, and it is difficult to get lost as long as you walk in a straight line, as the city is only a few hundred metres across. One major square has the cathedral which is impressive at street level, but high above there is a golden coloured dome that can be seen for miles out to sea.

If you prefer shopping then simply try going down the narrow lanes and you will soon find the shops. You might even come across a market to savour the smells of local fruit and cheeses and meats, but if that is not your scene then cafés and bars for a beer or tapas are everywhere.

The ship will offer a selection of tours and we have been on a couple over the years. On our first visit we went on a trip to the mountain village of Arcos de la Frontera. When I said mountain village, what I meant was a village perched on the top of a mountain. It is quite a large village with some 28,000 people living in it which swells by thousands more with tourists. Like so many of these places the houses are white making it beautiful from a distance and just as pretty when you walk around it. It is geared up for tourists and shops are always open when a coach arrives full of passengers with bulging wallets.

There are coach trips to other villages and they are often combined with a sherry tasting session or maybe a traditional lunch.

On another visit we had a simple walking tour of Cadiz to look at some of the streets and architecture. It was rounded off with an hour in a bar sampling the local sangria and tapas, and watching a flamenco demonstration. This is something I suggest you all try at least once as the atmosphere of a small crowded bar with loud guitar music and dancers stamping their feet is wonderful, and you may well find yourself joining in with the **"Oles!"** to get an encore.

Quite comprehensive walking tours of Cadiz are available, and knowing that a cruise fan will probably end up in Cadiz on a regular basis you can learn about the churches and museums or more interesting sights to go back and explore another time.

A visit to Cadiz can be a full day or just a short and sweet half-day stop, so you have a choice of how to spend the time. A trip on a coach to explore the city or further afield in Andalucia may be perfect, but Cadiz is so compact that you don't have to walk far to see a lot of different things. Of course it is also a port that you can decide to ignore and just stay on the ship and enjoy it when most passengers are away on their tours.

Malaga

Less than 100 miles from Gibraltar, and just a pleasant four to five hours sailing time, is the delightful port of Malaga.

We have visited and explored Malaga on two occasions with the first time in June 2003 aboard a ship called *Adonia*. As with the old *Arcadia*, she is no longer with the P&O fleet, and another ship with the same name is currently in service. For the confused, she was (or still is really) the sister ship of *Oceana* and we sailed on her in her maiden year with the fleet. There was a lot of publicity at the time as *Adonia* and *Oceana* were virtually identical and known as the White Sisters.

On the 21st June 2003 we had sailed by Gibraltar early in the morning and mid-morning there was a surprise as a helicopter flew above us filming. The captain (Rory Smith) eventually explained that we were about to sail alongside *Oceana* for a marketing video. The next half an hour was an amazing experience in our cruise adventures, being so close to a mirror image of ourselves. We could see and hear passengers on *Oceana* while the helicopter buzzed around capturing video footage from all angles.

Of course we couldn't resist buying a copy of this video when we got back home. It was called *'The White Sisters'* and our copy is now converted to DVD for occasional

Saturday evening viewing memories. It is rather special, as *Adonia* only stayed with P&O for two years before returning to Princess Cruises as *Sea Princess*. Coincidently she was brought into the fleet as a replacement during the period when the previous *Arcadia* became *Ocean Village* and the launch of the present *Arcadia* in 2005.

She was (still is no doubt) a lovely ship, as the loyal fans of *Oceana* prove.

...Time to return to Malaga

Sitting on the Costa del Sol, Malaga is the capital city of the Province with the same name. It is in the Spanish district of Andalusia and is the sixth largest city in the country. Malaga is one of the southernmost large cities in Europe and has a population of just fewer than 600,000. Its climate is wonderful, with winters often producing daytime temperatures above 20°C, and is extremely hot in the summer. This makes it very popular with the British and other Northern European holidaymakers.

First records show that it was a tribal community some 2,800 years ago and as with many Mediterranean cities Malaga has had an ever-changing history. Various armies have captured the city and influenced its development and cultures over the centuries. The Phoenicians arrived around 770 BC, and then it became a part of the Roman

Empire during the 1st century BC. There were several changes during the next 600 years before it was conquered by the Moors. Many of buildings have survived for hundreds of years, so the city has a mixture of architecture.

Now on that beautiful sunny day we eventually arrived in the port of Malaga just after lunch, and as it was short afternoon visit, we had no plans for a tour. Having studied the guide books, we decided to go and see the ruins of the Alcazaba Fort, as well as having a quiet walk around the city.

This was the moment where we first really did our own thing at a port. As we left the ship, we used the guide supplied on board to find our way through the city to the old Fortress. We had no knowledge of the Spanish language but after some initial concerns at the entrance box, tickets were bought and we walked (with smiles on our faces) up the slope of the hill leading to the way in. This may not sound a big deal but we had simply never attempted anything like it before.

Inside the fortress there was a time capsule of architecture with areas that had been preserved or restored to give the visitor a taste of fortress's history. Obvious changes in building styles could be spotted, particularly examples of Roman and Moorish influence. Distinct areas could be identified as living quarters or perhaps for cooking, and gardens had been recreated to show some of the plants that might have been there over the hundreds of years. Building materials changed, with the structure of walls being an obvious place to spot favoured materials and building styles of the various occupiers of the fortress and the city.

For the next hour or so we strolled around this intriguing site. At various points you can see over the walls with views of the city. From one spot we were able to look down towards the harbour and see our ship and the passengers leaving the dockside. They were being tempted by taxi drivers to save their energy in the seriously hot sunshine and some took up the offer or haggled with the driver of one of the many horse drawn carriages.

Suitably impressed with our little bit of cultural exploration, but extremely hot from a lack of shade, we decided it was time to move on and look around the shops of Malaga.

It was now that we discovered another cultural change in Spain... siesta time!

The shops of the city were closed and streets were almost deserted except for groups of tourists wandering up and down. Other than bars and cafés, most businesses were shut and local people had gone home to their air-conditioned homes to avoid the heat as they ate their lunch. At least we had a chance to admire the wide streets of the main shopping area with its marble (or similar) paving often shaded by huge canopies for some protection from the sun.

We window-shopped and eventually sat down at a street café for a delicious cup of coffee and rested our legs for a few minutes. It was obvious that by the time the shops came back to life again we would be exhausted from the heat so we strolled back towards the ship with a mental note to remember the siesta time on any subsequent visits.

So what else does Malaga offer to tempt the visitor?

Apparently shopping is really special if you time your visit right, but there are always organised tours from the ships taking passengers on coach, walking, and cycling tours of the city. There are museums to explore and of course there are several beaches nearby, but the more popular stretches of golden sand and calm sea are a few miles away. Transfers are usually available to take passengers to the resort of Torremolinos. For those wanting to see more of the area, there are trips to Marbella, and the adventurous passengers are sometimes offered horse rides in the mountains or kayaking in the sea.

+++

We went back to Malaga in July 2008 on board *Aurora*, and this time we had a full day visit allowing passengers a more comprehensive choice of tours. Once again we ignored the organised trips and did our own thing.

Deb and I had made plans to return to the Alcazaba Fort after really enjoying it so much the first time. Unfortunately it was Monday, and the site was not open to the public. We were left to wander the streets of the city, but at least the shops were open this time. Coffee and ice-cream had become a *must have* as we visited the ports of the Mediterranean, and Malaga did not let us down in this department.

It was hot again and we didn't walk for very long before the lure of air conditioning and a quiet ship tempted us back to *Aurora*. Sometimes it is good to make the most of a day in port and simply enjoy the choice of spots to stretch out on a lounger and occasionally cool down in a deserted pool.

I think if we ever go back again, a tour will probably be taken to enable us to look further afield at what Andalusia has to offer.

Almeria

Roughly a hundred miles east of Malaga there is another popular cruise ship stop at the port of Almeria. This city is the capital of the province of Almeria in the district of Andalusia, and at the time of our visits the city had a population of around 170,000. Just like Malaga, Almeria has had a mixed up history of invasions by various groups of people, and the city is dominated by a Moorish fortress called the Alcazaba on the top of a hill. Compared to the fortress in Malaga, this one is larger and is really impressive, especially being clearly visible from the port where we docked.

Also like Malaga we have had two visits here, on *Aurora* in 2008 and the following year on *Arcadia*, and yes this time it is the same *Arcadia* that sails in the fleet now.

Our first visit in July 2008 was on the way home from a voyage that had taken us as far as Istanbul. *Aurora* was being looked after by Captain Ian Hutley who was one of the more visible and outgoing masters of the ships that we have sailed on.

The all-day stop at Almeria gave the passengers a chance to stretch their legs before the final three days at sea as *Aurora* made her way back to Southampton. First impressions were not very good as it appeared to be a busy ferry port. Below us on the dockside there was a wire fence between our berth and a car park where there were several vehicles, full of mainly African families, waiting for a ferry going across the Mediterranean. Part of the car park was under cover, where a lot of the cars and vans were parked, but some chose (or perhaps were directed to) the outside section exposed to the sunshine that was already hot at 9:00 in the morning. Every vehicle seemed to have a full house of passengers but there were also bags and bags of clothes, food, material, and seemingly everything but the kitchen sink.

...well actually there might have been a couple of those as well.

We had no intention of going on any tours. We had spent a lot of money on trips already and we just wanted to have a walk and look around the city. We didn't rush to go ashore, as many passengers were on organised trips and they needed to get off the ship first. Our stroll to the city centre started with a long walk along the quayside past the car park of waiting ferry passengers and then out through the terminal gate.

Almost directly across the road from there was a large roundabout that had a long park running from it to both left and right. We went to the right and had a peaceful walk of a couple of hundred metres with areas of trees, hard-surfaced play areas and lakes. On either side of this park were busy roads but they were hardly noticeable.

After consulting our guide book we turned off to the left towards the shopping area along an avenue with a central pedestrian area with more trees, statues and fountains to give our cameras some exercise. I seem to remember that by the time we actually got to the shops we were almost exhausted. After all this was Spain and it was very, very, hot.

Our shopping was limited to an ice-cream and a bottle of cola to keep us going until we got home. I don't remember buying any souvenirs as our priority quickly became getting back to the cool ship. We were back on board before lunchtime and had a spell of sun-worship with the advantage of shade and a swimming pool to cool us down when necessary.

We spent much of the afternoon in our wonderfully cool cabin and I became amazed as I stared down from our balcony at the ferry car park where vehicles were still arriving. The car park was packed with cars and vans full of men women and children plus their carrier bags of supplies that were presumably not available in their native African towns. The covered area was completely used up and I felt so sorry for the children and old people struggling to stay cool out in the roasting sunshine.

They were still waiting to board their ferry when we left at 5:00 in the evening.

+++

With the knowledge we gained from this visit we were ready in July 2009 when we had another full day visit to Almeria. This time we arrived on the *Arcadia* that became one of our favourite ships in the fleet. We had a tour booked, and it was an early getaway on a coach towards the mountain village of Mojacar (pronounced ma-ha-ca).

This was a superb adventure.

The journey to Mojacar took quite a while and crossed a barren area known as the Desert of Tabernus. This was the location for many of Sergio Leone's series of Spaghetti Westerns starring Clint Eastwood (and others) during the 1960s. This is the only recognised desert in Europe, and as the name suggests, it is barren and has very little vegetation. There are a number of hills or little mountains, and one of these was our destination. As we got closer we could see the typically Mediterranean whitewashed buildings of the little town we were visiting.

Mojacar has taken great care to maintain its simplicity, and large vehicles are banned. Our coach dropped us off at the official parking spot some 100 metres from the town centre, and then it was immediately driven away to free up some of the limited space available. Our guide was an English lady who now lives and works in Spain, and she led us up the hill to what looked like the town square surrounded by cafés and shops with roads leading off in various directions.

Our walking tour started with a gentle stroll in a circuit around the lower section of the town, with a look at some Roman ruins, but I was just as thrilled by the narrow lanes with plant pots on the walls with trailing flowers just about everywhere. The locals left doors and gates open to give us glimpses of tiled courtyards with more flowering plants and the occasional cat sleeping in any shade they could find. The skies were pure blue and the sun was beating down on us.

After the gentle circuit of the town, our guide offered the group a chance to follow her up to a fortress area at the top of the town, or for the less energetic there was free time to grab a coffee or look around the shops. Deb and I were keen to see more of Mojacar so we joined a smaller group climbing up the steeper roads and lanes to the highest point of the town. It was a stunning view out across the desert as well as down on the rest of the town. With only a few of the group in tow we had a chance to talk to our guide more socially as well as learning about the area and the town itself.

Back down in the square we still had plenty of time by ourselves and we started with a cup of coffee. Somehow it was so much better than normal as we sat next to a set of railings overlooking the desert below. There were small doughnuts to nibble (or dunk) with our coffee and a little sparrow came and said hello to us in hopes of a titbit to eat. It eventually left quite happy after sharing our cakes. Our remaining time in the town allowed us to wander and take photos as memories of this beautiful place. A couple of souvenirs joined our collection and of course there was still a moment to enjoy an ice-cream.

When our guide got us together again we returned to the coach that had returned to collect us and there was an hour's drive back to the ship. The guide continued to give us facts and answer questions about Mojacar and Almeria, but many of us took the opportunity to doze.

Back on *Arcadia* we had a late lunch and then spent a couple of hours in Almeria itself to revisit the parks and to look around the shops.

The town of Mojacar was just one of the tours available. We have never been back to try out the other trips but most of the passengers appeared happy with what was on offer. One very popular trip was to a cowboy town film location that has been turned into a tourist attraction, with mock gunfights while visitors have a drink in the saloon bars.

Many passengers chose to join groups on a guided walk around the city of Almeria itself, and one of the walks also included a chance to sample local tapas. For the wine sampling fans there was a coach trip around the local area that included a visit to a vineyard. Other coach tours included a panoramic trip around the Andalusian countryside, and some went on a more focussed ride around the beautiful scenery of the Cabo De Gata Natural Park. Several of the more energetic ones chose a visit to a local Water Park for some excitement, while others simply went on a transfer to one of the nearby beaches.

Almeria has a lot to offer and I am sure most visitors can find something of interest to them.

Valencia

Carrying on around the coast of Southern Spain the next port we have visited is Valencia. We have only been there once, in June 2013 on board *Arcadia*.

Valencia is in the Spanish Region of the same name and is obviously its capital. It is the third largest city in Spain, after Madrid and Barcelona, and has one the busiest ports in the country, and possibly in Southern Europe. It has a population of around 800,000, and its history dates back to the Romans.

As this was our first visit we wanted to see something of the city, but this cruise had been one of relaxation after a hectic house move and so we kept our port visits simple. Rather than an organised tour we jumped on the shuttle bus which took us to the central area of the city and then we strolled and tried to get a sense of the place.

It is a big city and obviously busy, with serious traffic in the road where we were dropped off, but after five minutes of walking we found a quieter square with the Cathedral on one edge as well as a magnificent fountain and several statues to exercise our cameras. Many passengers were making their way into the Cathedral but we continued past the entrance and down a lane to explore further. This took us to another vast square where traffic was kept to the edges leaving a wonderful area to stroll, or to sit and chat with a cup of coffee as many of the local people were doing. While the locals waited for their buses to arrive to take them home, visitors strolled and admired the beautiful buildings or simply sat in one of the many cafés enjoying the wonderful sunny weather.

We moved on again down even narrower streets and discovered a market to explore. The smell of fresh fruit and flowers is delightful, although I personally find the aroma of strong cheeses and fish less pleasant. Around the outside of the market were smaller shops with some unusual produce. We had been looking for a tiled number that we could use for our new house and we found it here in the backstreets of Valencia. It was exactly what we wanted, but unfortunately we stupidly left it in a cupboard on the ship when we disembarked.

The city was very beautiful and while we only strayed perhaps 200 metres from the shuttle bus stop, we came across a lot to look at. The squares were vibrant with plenty of photographic opportunities, while the back streets were quiet, giving the visitor time to slowly explore the culture. Like so many of the cities we visit the architecture is stunning, but Valencia also has the obligatory bustling market, as well as several artisan shops to tempt you. I am sure that if we had walked deeper into the city we would have found lots more to interest us, but as I said, this cruise was all about relaxing and not so much about seeing things.

So our visit didn't last very long and after coffee and ice-cream we returned to the ship to enjoy the facilities of *Arcadia*. Many other passengers did take advantage of organised trips, and as usual I will give you a flavour of what was on offer.

Every port seems to offer tours that introduce people to the area and Valencia was no different, with trips advertised as '*Discover Valencia*' and '*Panoramic Valencia*'. The difference is that the Panoramic version tends to be more of a sit in the coach and see the sights with minimal walking, while the Discover one is more about stopping and walking around the attractions.

One trip was to see the porcelain factory in a nearby village where Lladro figurines are produced. Having barely heard of them, it was not on our list of *"what about this then?"*

The only other choice on this cruise was for a transfer to a local beach and these are often very popular. I grew up with a beach a couple of miles away so they don't mean much to me.

To be honest there wasn't a lot of choice but this was one of the first visits to Valencia by the P&O fleet, so no doubt more interesting and varied tours will be added to the list.

Barcelona

This is a city where we have enjoyed five visits over the years. We have been there on the previous *Arcadia* (2001), twice on *Oriana* (2002 and 2005), and twice on the present *Arcadia* (2010 and 2013). Barcelona is one of our favourite stops.

Barcelona is the second biggest city in Spain (only Madrid is bigger) with a population of some 1.6 million people. It is the capital city of the region of Catalonia and has a very busy cruise ship terminal that often has three or more large vessels in port at the same time. Barcelona is one of the popular ports to join a fly-cruise, with many major cruise lines using it regularly throughout the summer months.

It was founded by the Romans (they obviously liked Spain) and in the recent past was the venue for a Universal Exposition (EXPO) in 1929. Perhaps a little more memorable was that it hosted the Olympic Games in 1992. Both of these events were held close to Montjuic Hill from where you can look out across the city and see the major landmarks.

Our first visit to Barcelona was on that wonderful cruise back in 2001 on the old *Arcadia*. We explored on our own in the morning and then took a tour of the city sights in the afternoon.

Deb and I rarely go crazy and get off a ship as soon as the gangplank is open, but we were not very late that morning of 31st July 2001. With a tour waiting for us in the afternoon, we knew we needed an early start in order to get back to the ship in time for lunch. The shuttle bus left from very near the ship and took us over a large bridge that crosses the dock area before reaching the road system of the city. We were taken to a designated coach stop that was about 100 metres from the end of the famous avenue called La Rambla, with a tall statue of Christopher Columbus directly in front of us.

For those who have never been to La Rambla, it is a road with a pedestrian central area about 20 metres wide. There are numerous permanent shops and cafes but more interesting are the stalls and street theatre that make it both a crowded market and tourist attraction. By the time we got there it was packed with tourists from all over the world, alongside local people out shopping. There were all the usual fruit and vegetables stalls as well as flowers and souvenirs. Several artists drew sketches of anyone willing to pay, and others produced watercolour paintings of Barcelona landmarks. At the far end of the street market, some 200 metres away, there were even stalls selling pets.

On either side of this boulevard were busy roads and then shops, but one very special place about half way along is a permanent covered market known as La

Boqueria. If the area outside was busy, inside it was absolutely packed with shoppers. The market is divided into areas selling different products, and as you move around the smell in the air changes from fruit to sweets to flowers or cheese or sausages or fish, and everything looks gloriously fresh and tempting.

We had been warned to be careful while walking along La Rambla as there are a lot of pick-pockets and several gangs of conmen tempting unsuspecting strangers to try and win at dodgy card games. Over the years this crowded avenue has created thousands of insurance claims, but there seems to be no effort to stop the crimes other than a few police officers walking up and down. I have never seen a CCTV camera anywhere and if they are hidden away they do not provide any deterrent.

The morning flew by with the buzz of La Rambla, and we had a late lunch back on the ship, plus a short rest before we joined a coach for a panoramic tour of the city.

Our trip was primarily to show the major sights with very little walking involved, and it started with a drive along the waterfront to see the yachting marina and the modernised buildings. This was just a taster of the new city as soon we turned into La Rambla again and drove by the stalls and into the older parts of Barcelona. It wasn't long before we saw a strange building that looked like an apartment block carved out of a cliff. This was our first sighting of the buildings designed by Antoni Gaudi that confuse and amaze the viewers. They are a joy to see, and we now recognise his style in many Spanish cities.

Already thrilled with what we had seen we arrived at another Gaudi fantasy called La Sagrada Familia. This is a new cathedral that Gaudi designed. It is a gigantic construction project which began in 1892 and a projected completion date of 2040. We got off the coach here and had a few minutes to take a closer look at this amazing building, along with an interesting introduction by our guide.

When I described it as a fantasy I was not exaggerating. There is hardly a wall or feature that is the same as any other. It looks like a skeleton of a construction whose base level is once more like a rock out of which openings have been created that are doors, windows, and other areas with figures telling a story of religious themes. I apologise for not being able to describe it in depth because there is nothing quite like it, and I can only suggest going to see it, or at least find some photos of it to see my problem.

It is fantastic!

From La Sagrada Familia we had another ride on the coach to the area of Monjuic, passing much of the Olympic complex from 1992. It might be interesting to the sports fanatics to know that the stadium used was actually built for the 1936 Olympic Games. Unfortunately the Spanish Civil War meant the Games were transferred to Berlin, and it took Barcelona half a century to win the Games again. Our guide was happy to simply describe the main stadium as we passed by but many of us pleaded with her to see more of it. She reluctantly gave in to our demands and we stopped for ten minutes to take a peek inside.

...sensational!

Minutes later our coach started a steep climb to the gardens at the top of the hill known as Monjuic. This stunning high point is a park with lots of attractions such as the Spanish Village and Magic Fountain. To us on our first visit it was a series of areas with grassy patches, marble mosaics, majestic steps, statues and most importantly views down over the city. We could see our ship in one direction, and in the other La Sagrada Familia standing out of the heat haze that covered the city.

By the time we left this sensational park I felt totally gobsmacked by the experience of Barcelona. This had been a wonderful day from the moment we arrived at La Rambla, until we eventually arrived back on *Arcadia* late in the afternoon. We agreed that a return visit had to be high on our wish list.

+++

Well we did go back, and at the end of August in the following year (2002) we arrived on *Oriana*. The pair of us did different things in the morning, and while Deb went on a cycling tour of the city I joined a group of sports fans for a look at Barcelona's sporting venues.

Both trips lasted between two and three hours and Deb thoroughly enjoyed the experience of cycling around the city. The group rode through some of the quieter streets to the 13th-century Cathedral near the Picasso Museum, and then continued on to the Cuitadella Park. She was very impressed with the bikes and the organisation of the ride.

Meanwhile my coach trip to Sporting Venues turned out to be an hour wandering around the Barcelona's Nou Camp football ground. Yes it is a very special place and I enjoyed it, especially seeing a real European Cup in the trophy cabinet, but I was expecting more. I hadn't realised how important football is to the city. We did get a coach tour that drove by the Olympic Stadium again, but there was definitely no stopping this time. For footie fans it was superb, but the title of the tour was not clear that other sports are not seen as important in Barcelona.

I met up with Deb late in the morning and we had lunch together on *Oriana* before returning to the city in the afternoon. We went to La Rambla again and it was even more vibrant in the afternoon with the crowds being virtually all tourists as the locals had completed their daily shopping by then. It was noisier, with street theatre attracting small crowds at intervals along the boulevard. The popular attraction was human statues, with several people painted and dressed as marble monuments, cowboys, film stars, and even grotesque aliens. Of course the card-sharps were out in force fleecing money from naïve holidaymakers, and the number of artists sketching passers-by was much greater than we had seen before. With hundreds of tourists looking for memories, the stalls selling souvenirs were also doing a roaring trade.

La Rambla was as sensational as we remembered from the previous year and Barcelona had become a special place for us.

+++

In July 2005 we were on *Oriana* again for our third visit to this Spanish city. We made a serious mistake that day.

We had decided to walk from the shuttle bus stop to where we could catch the little funicular railway to the top of Monjuic again for a longer look around. Unfortunately the train was not in service and we made the stupid decision to walk up the hill instead. It was hot, far too hot for us especially as we were not prepared for the exposure with no drinks or hats. After an hour we were totally exhausted and it was getting close to us being ill. We were nowhere near the top and realised we had to turn back and get out of the sun quickly.

It was a bad morning and by the time we staggered back onto the ship we wrote off the rest of the day as we recovered. Lesson learnt, we will never try that again. In fact we have never been back to Monjuic again...

...so far anyway.

+++

Our fourth Barcelona visit was in July 2010 on board *Arcadia*. After our previous bad experience, we had a less stressful day: we simply went for a walk along La Rambla to soak up the atmosphere and do a little shopping. That was enough to bring the magic back, and the rest of the day was spent on the ship. Perhaps we should have done something different and there was (and still is) a good choice of organised activities and tours available.

There are various coach ride and exploration tours. One will always be the short introduction to the city at the major attractions, while others concentrate on Gaudi's architecture and another takes passengers to the old Gothic Quarter of Barcelona for a longer walking session. The bike rides are usually available as well as the Nou Camp Stadium experience, and then there is the trip to Monjuic.

For the beach lovers there is sometimes a transfer to Sitges a few miles away from the city. This is a major tourist seaside town that also hosts an annual film festival. Another trip takes groups by coach and train to nearby Montserrat for a look at the mountain area and the Benedictine Abbey.

Almost everybody can find something to interest them on a visit to Barcelona, either doing your own thing or getting to know the city and the surrounding countryside a little better.

+++

We have had one final stop at Barcelona in June 2013 on *Arcadia* again. As I said earlier, this cruise was all about having a break after our house move, and we avoided tours at all of the six ports we visited. So it was a trip on the shuttle bus and an hour in La Rambla for us.

There was a slight change from previous visits as a new bus and coach stop and parking area had been created. It was still close to the end of La Rambla, with the statue of Christopher Columbus looking down on us, so we weren't confused very much. Sadly we were a little disappointed with La Rambla this time as it has quietened down compared to how we remembered it. There were fewer stalls and less street theatre. The economic down-turn across Europe has had an effect on Barcelona and this street appears to have suffered. There were still lots of visitors enjoying its atmosphere but there was no longer the vibrancy that we remembered. Have we seen the best of this place, or will it grow again with the eventual financial recovery?

Well that is our cruising experiences of mainland Spain but there is one other place to cover before moving on to another country, and that is the island of Majorca.

Majorca

I think it only fair to point out that the island name is written as Mallorca by the Spanish and pronounced as Mayorca.

It is the largest of the Balearic Islands along with Minorca, Ibiza and Formentera. The island group is off the eastern coast of Spain with Mallorca about 150 miles east of Valencia. We have visited the island on four occasions, landing each time at the capital city of Palma. The island is perhaps 45 miles from north to south and 60 miles west to east. It is very popular with the people of Northern Europe for summer holidays. The island has a population of around 800,000 and half of them live in Palma.

Our first visit to Palma was in 2003 on the *Adonia* (the previous one) and we returned there in 2005 aboard *Oriana*, then in 2007 we were sailing on *Arcadia* (the current one), and most recently in 2011 it was on *Aurora*. We have never been on an organised tour and never strayed beyond the city. This might sound boring but many of the visits have just been for half days and we have never considered Mallorca as somewhere to explore beyond the city. Before you get the wrong impression, we really enjoy Palma and it is a sensationally beautiful city.

So how have we spent our time here?

Firstly we never have to rush and after watching organised tours disappearing on their coaches we amble down to the quayside and catch the shuttle bus to the centre of Palma. It is a long drive compared to some ports and on the way the road takes you around a hill that has an army barracks with old artillery guns pointing out to sea. At the end of this dock road, you join the major traffic route in and out of the city, and yes it is generally busy. The coach takes the cruise ship passengers along the Avenue Gabriel Roca for more than a mile. Your eyes will flash left and right now for several minutes as you pass wonderful buildings of all sizes and ages on the left and the marina to the right with hundreds of yachts, ranging from those for millionaires down to the average well-off man's weekend toy. There are cafés and bars where visitors and locals alike can sit and watch out for the famous while they eat their paella or tapas lunch with a coffee or glass of sangria.

There are often several cruise ships in port each day and the shuttle buses now turn to the right along a huge breakwater where buses stop and turn around. Many passengers will now see their floating homes across the harbour gleaming in the summer sunshine. This is also when the heat really kicks in, as there is no shade apart from the odd tree.

To get to the popular tourist sights, you have to walk back along the pathway towards the main road.

I hinted earlier that the roads are busy, and now you have to cross the main traffic route in and out of Palma. Pedestrians need to get across both of the carriageways which can take a minute or two, and unfortunately that gives plenty of time for passengers to start moaning. It is a fact of life that some cruise passengers love a good moan and here in Palma a couple of minutes to cross a road is a perfect excuse. Usually the subject of a moan is that *"It was never like this in the good old days"* or *"Why can't they drop us off closer to the centre?"*

There is however a good reason to get across the road, as above you is a little hill with the beautiful Cathedral of Mallorca next to the Almudaina Palace.

The cathedral is one of those buildings that are architecturally outstanding and pleasing to the eye. It is in the Gothic style and has pointed towers, ornate windows and flying buttresses plus multitudes of shapes that make the eye wander from area to area to pick out all the detail. Its construction was ordered by James 1st of Aragon in the year 1229 and it needed over 400 years to complete it. Work had to start again after an earthquake in 1851, and in 1901 even Gaudi had a say in the restoration although he walked away in 1914 after arguing with the builders.

The Almudaina Palace next door was an Arabian Fort and is more rectangular with square towers. During the 14th century it was claimed and restored by King James 2nd as his palace and nowadays is used by the Royal Family for state occasions.

These two buildings make a stunning view as you cross the busy road but before you get to them there is even more to see. First you arrive at a park with patches of grass or simple open areas but to the right of this is a huge lake with water features to wander around if architecture is not your thing. Walking on towards the cathedral complex there is an area where we have always encountered the living statues that are popular as street theatre in Spain. The pathway continues upwards now through a more shaded area with a long narrow pond that has fountains in the middle with trees and flowers to the sides making it like a little oasis in the hot sunshine conditions. The walls of the Almudaina Palace are to your right, and a smaller shaded pond is tucked away in a walled area. On our earlier visits we used to see a pair of black swans here. Finally you come out onto the open area with a road to the left and the huge palace building rises above you to the right.

Having made such a fuss about the splendour of the palace and the cathedral, I have to admit that we have never gone inside either of them for a look around. They delight us with their external magnificence as we pass by on our way to the shopping areas and squares of the city.

So a gentle stroll from the cathedral area down a few narrow streets and you arrive at the shopping area and eventually a large square. Around the square there are various places to sit with a coffee or a glass of beer watching the world pass by, or admiring the architecture. To one side is an impressive government building with flags above and guards on the doors, and nearby there is a Gaudi masterpiece to confuse your thoughts. Assuming it is still there, a very old olive tree gives shade and somewhere to sit on the benches near it. From that square the lanes take you further into the shopping area with places to look at or buy clothes, sweets, souvenirs or something for a snack.

We have even found a supermarket to stock up on *nice-to-haves* for the cruise and it had a market down below where we have bought local bits and pieces as memories of Palma. The last time we had a stop in Palma the recession was obvious with far fewer shops and market stalls, but that could change again in a short space of time as Europe eventually makes a recovery.

The only time we explored the city a little further was on a hop-on-hop-off bus, and that was a real treat as we saw so much more but at little cost. These open-topped buses are popular with tourists all over Europe, and are a very cost-effective way of seeing somewhere for the first time and to spot a likely place to spend more time at. Many, like us, simply stay on the bus for its complete circuit giving us a panorama of the city and mental notes made to perhaps visit somewhere later in the day or on a future visit.

If you want an organised tour to see more of Palma or the island, then several options are available from the ship. Here is a flavour of what you might like to try from our latest trip to Mallorca:

There was a coach tour described as the Best of Palma, and another looking at Scenic Mallorca. For the more energetic there was a bike ride of the Old Town within Palma.

A trip away from the city was to the Caves of the Dragon (Cuevas del Drach) near the harbour resort of Porto Cristo on the eastern side of the island. Another tour was to the resort of Soller on the North West coast of the island. This included a ride on an old wooden train to look at the countryside.

The ships offer a varied programme for tours at all of their stops and there is usually something for everybody if that style of exploration suits you.

Other Spanish Ports

Cruise companies are always trying to find new ports to visit to give passengers more variety. It might also be a clever way of getting ports to compete with each other to attract ships, and that may mean cheaper berthing fees.

Over the recent years a couple of new ports have been added to the Spanish list but we have not been to them as yet. Hence I cannot give any details from personal experiences but I have included them to keep the story as up to date as possible.

Cartagena
This is a city in the regional province of Murcia and is situated on the south eastern coast between Almeria and Valencia. It has a population of over 200,000.

Cartagena is a city where lovers of museum and all things historical are going to be in their element. There is a Roman Amphitheatre to look at and several museums covering all kinds of topics and archaeological treats to keep you occupied. If architecture and culture is not high on your wish list, there is always the chance to do a little shopping.

The usual tourist buses are there to tempt you but an alternative is the local water craft tours.

Alicante

Here is another city on the south east coast of Spain, this time in the district of Valencia. Alicante is the capital city within the province of the same name and obviously has a port on the Mediterranean Sea. Geographically it is between Cartagena and Valencia. Its population is approaching 350,000 people who rely heavily on tourism for the economy of the city.

Mount Benacantil overlooks the city and has the Santa Barbara Castle as somewhere to explore. Down in the city there is a palm tree lined avenue called Esplanade de Espana to stroll along on its patterned paving. There are various museums to absorb some of the history and culture of the city, and the usual selection of cafés and bars to relax in. Of course there are plenty of shops to spend your Euros as well.

Alicante sits on the Costa Blanca and close by there are some beautiful beaches (Playa) that are popular all year round, with the climate warm in the winter and hot in the summer.

+++

That just about covers the ports that P&O visit on the Spanish coastline. There are only a finite number of places that cruise ships can visit as they have to have a dockside big enough to land at, or at least a safe sheltered bay where the ships can anchor and take passengers ashore in their tenders. Looking at the coastline there are not that many ports left but the remaining three Balearic Islands might attract some attention in the future.

I have no information on where other cruise lines land but I am quite confident that they will be visiting the same ones as P&O.

Organised tours, or plan your own visits?

If you look at forums that are popular with frequent cruisers, one of the regular questions concerns booking tours. It is clear that there are some quite differing views about booking tours through the cruise company, or doing your own thing at each port.

You don't have to go on tours that the ship offers, and it is quite simple to look online to find alternatives before you sail from Britain. There are even reputable companies throughout the world that will find and book tours for you which are organised according to the ship's itinerary and the time a ship will spend in each port.

There is also no need to pre-book any tours at all, as you can simply get off the ship and book a taxi to take you to somewhere you want to look at. Alternatively you can catch a hop-on-hop-off bus for tours of the cities, and at most ports there will be companies at the terminal offering tours to the best attractions.

So although I may appear to be suggesting there is no need to buy the tours on board your ship, hundreds of passengers do use this service. So what is the best thing to do?

Buying tours on board the ship

Disadvantages:

To be quite frank about ship-organised tours, they are usually more expensive than booking a similar one direct with a local tour company.

People are employed on the ships to sell the tours, and they have to be paid. The onshore companies have agents who work with the coach and guide companies to organise the tours, and they too need to be paid. The actual tour companies know they will almost always have a guaranteed market from the ships, so they possibly charge more.

So by the time the passenger has bought a tour, the price will have risen to cover all the extra people involved, and the possible hiking of prices by the tour companies.

On an organised tour there is little or no flexibility and you have a set time at each location, even though you might want to spend longer looking at something really special to you.

The mix of people on the tour may be such that you end up with some people who are slow at walking, meaning the guide has to tailor the pace of the tour accordingly. This is not a dig at those people struggling to walk fast, but just an issue that is quite common with older age profiles of cruise passengers.

Some tours can leave you feeling like sheep – herded en masse from one spot to another

Advantages:
The end product is probably a well tried and tested one. The tour may have been used before, and the feedback for it had to have been good to allow it to be sold again. Coaches are of a good standard, and guides are used that can speak English.

Tours can be quite imaginative sometimes, including such things as lunch at a local farm to sample true regional food.

Someone is organising everything for you, and if something is not to your liking, you can complain directly to the people on board who cannot get away from you.

This next point is the really important one: if something goes wrong on a tour organised by the ship, such as the tour overrunning or a coach breaking down, the ship will not set sail and leave you behind.

Doing your own thing

Advantages
- You will probably spend less.
- The taxi driver might turn out to be a dream and not only takes you to where you want to go, but offers to act as a guide for a small charge.
- If you are using a hop-on-hop-off bus it may well highlight somewhere really special to look at so you can stop and spend time there before catching the bus again later.
- You can be flexible with where you go and how long you spend at a location.

Disadvantages
Even with the best possible planning, it can all go horribly wrong.

- The tour you have booked privately may not be with a reputable company and not worth the money, or worse still is a con-trick.
- The taxi driver may be less than honest, and overcharges or leaves you stranded miles from nowhere.
- You might get confused with bus times and miss connections to get you back to the ship in time to sail.
- If you miss the advertised sailing time, the ship has no obligation to wait and could set sail for the next

port without you. You have to hope your insurance policy will cover the problem.

It's your holiday – and your choice!

So I know I haven't given you a satisfactory answer, and to be honest, there probably isn't an answer that suits everyone.

One suggestion I would offer is to take care in any new port, especially if there might be a language issue. In these situations we tend to book a tour via the ship and use it to check out what we want to see more of, and go there ourselves on our next visit.

On the other hand if you have been somewhere several times and know what you want to do, it would be silly not to at least check out the options before you leave home. The savings made by doing your own thing at two or three familiar ports may well pay for that on-board organised one somewhere new to you.

Well that is enough about tours and let's get back to the ship as we sail away from Spain and the coast of France beckons.

France

Back in 2001 when we explored the western Mediterranean on *Arcadia* (the previous one), we sailed beyond the Spanish coastline and started to pass by France. This country might be quite large but only a little bit of it lies on the Mediterranean Sea. Over the years we have visited four ports and we have only returned to one of them.

Marseille

At the end of July 2001 we arrived aboard the old Arcadia at the port of Marseille which is a sea journey of a little over 200 miles from Barcelona.

Marseille is the second largest city in France (after Paris) and has a population of around 850,000 people. It is the largest French port and is important for its commercial container business, as well as for fishing. The city itself has the usual mix of architectural styles which are a result of a history of occupation by different armies and people over the centuries.

As well as our visit in 2001 we returned there in 2010 on board the current *Arcadia*.

On Monday the 30th July 2001 we arrived in the port of Marseille at breakfast time. Actually we had already finished our breakfast by that time, as we had a tour booked. So by 8:15am we were in the Palladium Theatre to get our little stickers to identify the group we were with. Our tour was called *'The City of Marseille'* and began with a coach trip into the older part of the town before starting a walk to look at some of the city's history. Apart from tall buildings I remember very little about the coach ride except for the guide pointing out a poster on a wall showing Zinedine Zadine (born in Marseille) who was a very popular French footballer at that time but who became rather infamous for head-butting an opponent in a World Cup Final.

We drove along the sea front and the guide pointed out a little island called '*If*' that was a short distance from the shore. There is a prison fortress on the island called Chateau d'If that was used during the films of '*The Count of Monte Cristo*' and '*The Man in the Iron Mask*'. I have to admit not having seen either of these films. To be honest I was more impressed with the grand hilltop Palais du Pharo which was built for the Emperor Napoleon III. Even more embarrassing now, the only Napoleon that I was aware of was called Bonaparte, and it was only many years later that I realised my error.

It wasn't long before we were dropped off to start our walk taking us from an area in the Old Town down towards the Old Harbour. The busy city seemed eerily quiet as most of our route was spent in narrow lanes with tall buildings on either side, but at least we were in the shade, and away from the heat. We made our way down several flights of steps, and the guide was doing a good job at keeping us moving. It was difficult to get all the facts about the buildings we passed but I did remember some of the descriptions that the guide was giving us.

One sprawling cluster of buildings and courtyards in the Old Panier Quarter of the city attracted my attention. This was La Vielle Charité which started out as a hospital for the destitute but eventually became a museum. It has a rather beautiful three-storey galleried walkway around a central courtyard, and a superb ovoid shaped dome on a chapel roof.

When we arrived at the waterfront again the coach driver took pity on our aching feet and we had a ride towards the city's Neo-Byzantine Cathedral known as the Basilica de Notre Dame de la Garde. It is up on the highest point of Marseille and as well as being visible from miles away, is a rather special building. Externally it has a huge dome and also a square bell tower with a belfry that supports a 30-feet high statue of the Madonna and Child which is covered in gold leaf. Inside, the cathedral is a mix of gold leaf and stonework that appears to be red and white stripes.

Being a non-believer I don't spend much time in religious buildings. Yes I find them totally beautiful and architecturally wonderful, but I feel uncomfortable clumsily invading a place that is special to so many people. I am much happier just looking at the outside views and leaving the inside to those with faith.

The last place I remember from that day was the Palais Longchamp. As a building it now houses a museum, but the impressive bit is the monument in front of it which is a huge fountain surrounded by statues and arches. It is a water feature to thrill a visitor and I spent ages taking photographs of the water as it spouted and trickled and flowed.

+++

Well that was the end of the tour on our first visit, but we returned there in 2010 on one of our many cruises on the new *Arcadia*. That day was much more relaxed and all we did was catch a shuttle bus to the Old Harbour area and began our day with a stroll along the sea front. That led us to a market where we browsed for a while. Strangely, with so much to see in this city we didn't stay too long and were soon back on the ship.

There were lots of tours we could have joined including a simple ride on the *'Little Train'* for a different view of the city.

Further afield there was a coach trip to look around the nearby countryside and the town of Aix En Provence. Alternatively there were two tours going to the town of Avignon. One was a simple panoramic trip where we could have sung that childhood favourite...

"Sur Le Pont, d'Avignon

On y danse, On y danse....."

...while the other tour included a visit to the village of Chateau Neuf du Pape for a glass of wine.

The final option was a tour of the countryside which took people to the hilltop town of Le Castellet and the nearby seaside beach of Bandol.

My long-lasting memory of that day was that we were late leaving due to the Mistral winds that were making the sea conditions rough. We had had sunshine all day but the wind was getting stronger creating high waves that were running across the harbour exit. Captain Ian Walters delayed departure because the conditions were making it tricky to get out of the harbour without being smashed against the walls. We were actually having dinner when the ship finally left Marseille, and the Captain warned us that it might be a bit bumpy as we rounded the breakwater. The ship was actually travelling quite quickly by the time we went through the harbour exit and then we were pushed sideways by the wind. The violent movement made many of the diners gasp...

...but any disturbance from the unusual movement was just temporary and we quickly returned to our food.

Toulon

In August 2002 we were sailing on *Oriana* for the second time and arrived at the port of Toulon. It is less than 100 miles along the coast from Marseille and is a much smaller city with a population in the region of 170,000 people. Toulon is a naval base and the port is busy with some of the larger French navy ships.

Oriana was being captained by Hamish Reid, and we had just had a busy few days of tours which might be why this city didn't really inspire us very much. Our first views were of a cityscape of high-rise apartment blocks with a pretty series of hills in the distance. The tours being offered by the ship did not appeal to us, with the majority taking passengers around the surrounding Provence area to the town of Aix or the resort town of Bandol. There were no tours of Toulon itself, which would have been our preferred option.

We went for a walk to explore the city.

The weather wasn't helping our impressions either, as this was one of the rare days in nearly 300 days of cruising where it was dull and drizzly. Our walk took us along the dockside and then into the back streets and market squares. One of our finds was a small square with the rather pretty Municipal Opera House fronted by a façade of balconies, towers and arches. A statue stood a few metres in front of the building that was unusually not of Christopher Columbus. The name on the plaque unfortunately didn't really explain his significance.

We were dressed as if it was a typical Mediterranean day and the drizzle was making us damp by now. Undeterred, we strolled down more of the narrow streets between three-storied and four-storied houses with shutters on their windows and an abundance of Juliet balconies. Around a corner we discovered a large statue with a water feature. It was called *The Fountain of the Three Dolphins*, but the carved creatures were not obviously dolphins, and we decided it was more like *The Fountain of the Three Cod*.

I am sure the people of the city are proud of their home and have lots to offer to visitors. If it had been a sunny day we might have explored further and enjoyed ourselves, but on this occasion Toulon didn't work for us.

Damp and a little disappointed, we made our way back to the ship.

Oriana has lots of places where you can relax on a damp day and simply read a book over a cup of coffee or people-watch. There is always an afternoon Individual Quiz in the Lords Tavern, and a chance to enjoy a beer before a delicious dinner.

We avoided that evening's cabaret, which featured Renato Pagliari of the 1980's duo Renee and Renato. I never did like them, and *'Save Your Love'* is a song that features highly on my ***"yuk"*** list.

The resident band (Natural High) was always a good alternative in Harlequins Bar followed by a late snack and a cup of hot chocolate up in the Conservatory before bedtime.

Cannes

July 2005 and we were back on *Oriana* again under the control of Captain Mike Carr for the third of the French ports that we have so far visited.

Cannes on the Mediterranean coast of France has a population of less than 200,000 but is packed each summer with holiday makers as well as the rich and famous who go there to be seen as well as enjoying the wonderful sunshine. It is one of those places that people know about even if they have never been there.

Every May it holds the famous Cannes Film Festival at the Palais des Festivals, which is just a short walk from the Old Port. Even when the festival is long over, tourists flock to the theatre to look at the grand steps leading up to the entrance. There is one set painted red to allow photographs to be taken as if standing on a red carpet. Near the entrance in the floor tiles you can see handprints of famous actors and actresses spanning time back to when the festival started. To add to the magic there is an avenue of palm trees to walk along and look out for celebrities.

There is also a beautiful sandy beach to enjoy the warmth and to stare out at the Mediterranean.

Arriving at Cannes on a cruise ship is different to the places I have described so far. Only the smallest ships can actually dock at this little port. *Oriana* is not large by today's standards but she had no option but to anchor in the bay a little way from shore.

This is a tender port.

To many seasoned cruisers this is a delightful moment as it means that the ship uses it lifeboats as what are referred to as tenders, and passengers are taken ashore in them. Yes it takes time to get on board the little boats and ride to shore, and it all takes a lot longer than walking down the steps straight onto the dockside. But that ride to shore is exhilarating. You are close to the sea and can feel the waves hitting the hull and bouncing the craft around. A modern cruise ship does not get moved around unless the sea is extremely rough, so a tender ride is a chance to really experience the strength of the waves.

Anyway, we had a morning tour that was taking us to Nice for a panoramic look at the area plus a ride on the 'Little Train' to explore the city. Our trip ashore was smooth with hardly any waves to worry us and we were soon on a coach for the drive along the coast to Nice.

We got off the coach on the Promenade Des Anglais overlooking the sensational golden sands of the beach. The Promenade Des Anglais is a busy road with a wide pavement along the sea front overlooking the Baie des Agnes (Angel Bay). The pavement is wider than the road, allowing hundreds of people to stroll without being crowded. There is also a cycle path, which is wider than whole pavements in most British towns.

While the guide got our tickets for the Little Train, we had a few minutes to look at the hundreds of sunbathers, as well as the more energetic swimmers.

Once comfortably aboard the white train we set off along the avenue with the carriages clanking and the bell being rung enthusiastically. We were attracting waves and smiles from the people we passed as we rumbled along the busy avenue. After a while we turned off from the busy road and continued our tour along a quieter road behind the seafront buildings. There were plenty of wonderful buildings to look at before we started to climb up a hill with views of a park, and the city's war memorial. At the top of the hill was a coach park where we joined several other little trains that were stopped, and we had a chance to buy a drink and explore the area. It seems these parks always have a statue, and once again it was of Christopher Columbus.

This was our chance for a walk around with sensational views over the city of Nice from the Colline de Chateau (Chateau Hill). Our cameras focussed down to the old town area of Nice, capturing the buildings with their pastel-coloured walls and red tiled roofs. The busy cityscape gave way to the golden sands of the beach, and then the blue of the sea faded gently into the similarly blue sky.

Our refreshment break was over and we jumped back on the train to rattle and rumble our way down again past small waterfalls and the ruins of an old cathedral, and then soon we were back to where we started. There was a short wait for our coach, so we took a final look at the wonderful seafront before having another panoramic ride back to Cannes.

My memory blurs now, and I am not sure if we went back to *Oriana* for lunch and then returned ashore, or if we simply stayed ashore after the coach trip. Whenever it was we walked a short distance to the Palais des Festival and posed for each other to take a photo of us sitting on the red carpeted steps. We looked at the hand prints of Clint Eastwood and Sophia Loren, among others, and even Mickey Mouse has a permanent reminder of his paws.

Along with hundreds of others we strolled along the palm tree-lined avenue and stared at a statue of George Pompidou set among the flowers and bushes. The vast beach was of similar golden sand to that in Nice, and even in the middle of summer it was far from crowded. Just a little way off-shore we could see the familiar and beautiful sight of our ship with its yellow ochre-coloured funnel.

The afternoon brought a change in the weather, and although the sky remained clear and the sun shone, the wind was becoming noticeable, and then annoyingly stronger, blowing the sand up into our faces. We joined the queue for our tender boat back to *Oriana,* but our ride back was very different to the earlier experience. The waves lifted us and tossed the boat around and we bumped our way back with spray continually flying over the top of our craft. It was exciting, as I could feel the strength of nature and yes, I admit to being relieved as we were carefully assisted off the bouncing tender and back onto our ship. Later we heard that the captain had had to decide if it was safe to use the tenders and considered abandoning attempts to return her passengers. The alternative plan would have involved bussing those passengers still ashore to our next port, but fortunately as the afternoon wore on the sea conditions improved enough to avoid this extreme situation, and before dinner everyone was safely aboard and *Oriana* was moving on.

As well as our trip on the little train in Nice there were various tours to tempt us. Another trip to Nice included a visit to an open air market, while others went to look around Monaco, St Tropez and Monte Carlo. These are rather special tours visiting some of the most spectacular places along the coast of Southern France.

Calvi (Corsica)

At the end of August in 2002 we arrived at the last of the French Mediterranean destinations we have sampled. This was at the small town of Calvi situated on the north-western Corsican coast. Calvi has a population of five or six thousand people and is famous for supposedly being the birth place of Christopher Columbus.

The island of Corsica is geographically less than 10 miles north of the Italian island of Sardinia, separated by the Strait of Bonifacia. It is split into two districts with the north being known as the Haute-Corse (Upper Island) with the south being Corse-du-Sud (Lower Island). Corsica is about 110 miles north to south, and some 50 miles west to east and has a population of around 300,000. The town of Ajaccio in the south is famous as the birthplace of Napoleon Bonaparte.

Returning to the town of Calvi, it has a small harbour which was not big enough to allow Oriana to dock, so Captain Hamish Reid anchored our ship in the bay and passengers were tendered to and from the shore. Our first impressions were very positive with a vista of mountains in the distance behind the little town. From the deck we could also see a tempting Citadel built into the rock and looking like a fortress. It overlooked the harbour and faced out towards us in the bay.

We had decided that this was where we would be heading.

Once the tour groups had left the ship we queued for a tender and were soon on our way towards the harbour for a couple of hours exploring. Calvi is split into two areas with the Citadel being part of the Upper Town, and the Lower Town below made up of the bulk of the housing plus the harbour and shopping areas. We had a map to help us but it not really necessary, and we were soon strolling up the road toward the Citadel. To our left was a rock face occasionally covered in trailing flowers while on the other side was the cliff overlooking the sea. There were some rough paths leading down the cliff where locals obviously took short cuts to beaches through a forest of giant cactus plants, which all had tall spikey stems and flowers, and would have taken no prisoners. The cactus leaves were enormous and many had names carved into them and love pacts between youngsters whose scratched names would probably survive for many years.

Out in the bay we could see *Oriana,* with hills in the distance again. Deb and I walked up the winding cliff road until the rooflines of the buildings inside the fortress walls were visible. We reached the Citadel gateway and took a peek inside at the houses and occasional shops. They were designed to attract tourists, but we weren't overly interested in what we saw. Satisfied with our little adventure we returned down the hill past the *man-eating* cacti and some beautiful flowers.

While we spent a few minutes looking round the shops of the Lower Town before returning to *Oriana*, many of our fellow passengers had chosen from the available tours. There was a variety of coach tours and walks around the villages and towns of the island. We hadn't chosen a tour, but in hindsight I think we made a mistake as, to date, this was the only time we visited Corsica. *Oriana* was anchored here all day with a late evening departure and there was plenty of time for a tour of the island as well as our look around Calvi.

This is without doubt a pretty island with some lovely beaches to spend some time on. There are also numerous intriguing towns to look at, along with a nature reserve in the mountains in the centre of the island.

Fortunately the sun shone all day, so we enjoyed the chance of a quiet ship to soak up the tanning rays, and made the most of a quiet swimming pool and plenty of loungers to relax on.

+++

That is the last of the French ports that we visited over our cruises around the Western Mediterranean. Without a doubt Marseille is an impressive city and needed more time to explore. On the other hand Toulon just didn't do it for us.

Cannes was sensational and is a perfect port to explore several of the fashionable and celebrity-popular towns of Nice, Monaco, and the beach resorts of the French Riviera. The island of Corsica was delightful but we missed out on so much by not exploring beyond the small town of Calvi.

Italy

It's time to sail on across the Mediterranean past Spain and France and arrive in Italy.

This is our favourite country in the Mediterranean and is the dividing point between the western and eastern areas of the sea. It has wonderful places to visit on its western coast, as well as several islands. On the eastern side there is the delicious city of Venice that I will not talk about in this book, but if you want to know about our trips there, try reading A Cornishman Cruises to Venice.

We have both said that if leaving Britain permanently was an option, then Italy would be high on our list of places to settle. Our love of its culture, food, and history has increased over the years, and it even inspired us to learn a little bit of the language.

I will start in the north-west of the country, and a port we have not visited but which is increasingly becoming a popular one: Genoa.

Genoa

OK so we have never been to Genoa, and in fact we had never seen it on an itinerary on any of the cruises that we considered over the last few years. It is however quite an important port now as in 2014 P&O joined the Mediterranean fly-cruise market and Genoa became a regular stop and a terminal point where cruises start and finish. So I thought it only fair to spend a few minutes looking at this city in the north-west of Italy, and the closest to the ports of France that we have just finished with.

Genoa is 200 nautical miles north-east from Marseille so is just an overnight trip for a modern cruise ship. The city of Genoa is in the region of Liguria and is the largest sea port in Italy and the sixth largest city in country, with a population of a little over 600,000. It is around 250 miles west of Venice, a similar distance north of the capital city of Rome, and just 70 miles south of Milan.

It is a city that is commercially busy, but also has a multitude of places for the tourists to visit and enjoy. It is also renowned to be the birthplace of Christopher Columbus...

...wait a minute, wasn't he supposed to have been born in Corsica??

There are either several famous people called Christopher Columbus, or there is a lot of confusion about where he arrived into this world.

Anyway, what can a P&O cruise ship passenger get up to if they land in Genoa and buy a tour from the ship?

Well, first of all there is the usual tour of the city which combines a coach drive with some walking at the more popular sights. There is free time built in to allow people a chance to explore on their own for a little while and find some souvenirs.

Rather than a coach trip, one tour takes the passengers on a trolley train to look at the highlights.

Genoa has one of the largest aquariums in Europe and of course this is one of the trips on offer.

If you want to go a little further afield, there is a tour around the Ligurian coast to look at fishing villages and the beautiful clear waters in the numerous bays. Maybe a chance to go wine tasting might be an interesting alternative morning out. Another option is a transfer to Milan where you can have a few hours to explore on your own, or maybe take a trip down the coast a little way to the charming resort of Santa Margherita.

If all else fails then the ship will take you to a local beach to let you relax there for a few hours before collecting you later.

Of course you could do your own thing. Take a look online before you leave home or buy some guide books to research the city. It will be much cheaper to target what you want to see and then take a taxi to whatever takes your fancy. Failing everything else, simply jump on the hop-on-hop-off bus and see what Genoa has to offer.

Santa Margherita

As I said, we have never visited Genoa but not much more than 20 miles south is the small port and town of Santa Margherita in the same Liguria region of Italy. We have been to this port on three occasions and the first time was Sunday 29th July 2001 aboard the old *Arcadia*. As I have already said, this was a superb cruise and we visited many wonderful places.

Santa Margherita is little more than a fishing harbour and certainly not large enough for *Arcadia* to dock, so Captain Reid dropped the ship's anchors a little way offshore before 8:00 in the morning. It being a tender port, the lifeboats were soon being lowered into the water and made ready to take passengers ashore. We had a tour booked that morning but there was time to stand on the promenade deck and look at the scenery before we had to get ready.

The town looked beautiful in the early morning sunshine. We could make out the dockside where there was a beach to one side with coloured parasols ready for locals and tourists alike to enjoy the golden sands. A road appeared to run from one end of the town to the other just behind the waterfront, and beyond that we could see a few rows of buildings. Santa Margherita is built at the foot of a hill with lush vegetation and the occasional villa for the better-off residents. One or two church towers and steeples rose above the houses, while a fortress to one side of the harbour was the only reminder that this was another Mediterranean region that had been fought over by various armies for several hundreds of years.

After breakfast we collected our tour stickers and queued for the tender ride to shore. It was a lovely sunny morning and the short ride on our little boat heightened our anticipation for the day. When we arrived on the dockside the scene was even more spectacular with houses, offices, and shops no more than the width of the road away. These buildings were a mixture of three, four, or even five stories and all painted in the typically Mediterranean pastel shades. Narrow streets led away into the little town, but there was no time to explore as our tour was not going to look around Santa Margherita.

We assembled on the quayside for a few minutes until the tour guides gathered their particular groups together. A young Italian lady called for all of us on tour D to follow her and get on board a local pleasure boat. We were going for a scenic trip around the coast to the stunning little fishing village of Portofino.

Our boat ride was a delightful half-an-hour spent looking at the beautiful coastline of woodlands with stunning houses dotted among them. Our guide described what we were seeing, and let us know that the villas poking out of the trees belonged to the rich and famous. She also introduced us to Portofino, explaining that it is a protected area with severe limitations on the number and size of boats entering the harbour.

Eventually we turned into a bay and then ahead of us was the wonderful sight of Portofino. I come from Cornwall where there are scores of picturesque fishing villages, but this was in a different league. First there were houses clinging to a cliff that was covered in flowering shrubs, and then came the harbour-side buildings that were so colourful with shades of yellows, pinks, and oranges that made us all smile and get our cameras out.

Portofino is a magnet for the beautiful and powerful people of the world who have serious bank balances. They come here to enjoy the stunning atmosphere, but also to be seen as they peruse the designer label boutiques before sipping coffee on the waterfront, and looking out across the harbour crowded with millionaires' yachts. As we left our pleasure-craft it was if I was stepping into a fairy-tale village and I instantly felt that it was going to be a really special day.

Assembled as a group on the tiny pebbled beach, our guide explained what we would be doing and told anyone wishing to do their own thing to be sure to be back on time at the agreed spot for our trip back. Deb and I had no immediate plans to break away on our own so we followed her up a little lane.

The first stop was the church of St George...the same St George as our own patron saint. It was Sunday and we could not go in as a service was in progress, but the architecture and a beautifully carved door kept our cameras busy as our guide explained a little of its history. To one side of the church was a flagpole with the cross of St George fluttering in the gentle breeze. From there we turned down a lane and passed by sensational views out over the sea and several stunning villas.

Our group had a mixed age profile and the guide was ensuring everyone was keeping up and could hear her as she introduced us to the highlights. Deb and I struggled with the slow walking pace and after a few minutes of frustration we escaped and made our own way along the rest of the lane to enjoy the scenery.

With our cliff top walk completed we retraced our steps to the harbour and walked up a side road to look at the shops. This was when we realised just how expensive this little town is. Yes the clothes were really special and the prices reflected their designer labels, but the prices were far beyond our budget, so we restricted ourselves to looking in the souvenir outlets for a memory to take home. Our ice-creams were also expensive but the taste was sensational and so refreshing on such a hot morning.

By 12:00 noon our group were back on the beach, carrying tired cameras and carrier bags full of goodies. To round off the morning we had a musical show from the bells of a little church near the harbour. It had been a lovely morning and as we sat on our boat returning to Santa Margherita, the majority of us had smiles on our faces as we looked at the cliffs again, and sipped a drink supplied by our guide.

Back in Santa Margherita we had the chance to look around the town but most of us quickly joined the queues for the tender boats back to *Arcadia*. It had been several hours since we last ate and our stomachs were demanding food. With hindsight, perhaps we should have come back after lunch and explored the town, but we were tired, and happy with what we'd seen and done, so simply enjoyed the afternoon on a lounger by the swimming pool.

+++

The following year (Sunday 25th August 2002) we were back at Santa Margherita, this time on board *Oriana* captained by Hamish Reid. It was tempting to go to Portofino again but we decided to be a little more adventurous. We took the ship's tender to shore and then turned right onto the road towards the town of Rapallo that we had been told was just a twenty minute walk away...

...that was a serious underestimate!

It was perhaps three miles from the harbour dockside to the centre of Rapallo and it took us nearly an hour to walk. Of course the weather was hot and sunny, and by the time we arrived at the waterside in the town of Rapallo we were exhausted.

Rapallo is a much bigger town than Santa Margherita and very much a tourist resort with a marina, shops and beaches to enjoy. We walked along the seafront, found another statue of Christopher Columbus pointing to something, and then arrived at a more commercial area. As well as a few shops we came across a street market that included antique sellers. There were lots of lovely fruit and vegetables and bargain bits of furniture, but we were in no mood to go carrying things back to the ship.

After an ice-cream we felt ready for the return journey and walked back to Santa Margherita. I think we were warmed up by now and the walk didn't feel quite as exhausting. We spent a little more time looking at the buildings, and were fascinated by some of the facades that had painted panels to brighten up a possibly boring wall. Elsewhere another fun sight was scaffolding with a screen that had pictures of a house printed on it. From a distance it looked like a real building.

Once back at the harbour of Santa Margherita we headed straight to the tender queue and bobbed up and down on the short journey back to *Oriana*'s air conditioning and our fridge with its plentiful supply of cold drink.

Later, we gave our brains a bit of exercise with the individual quiz in the Lord's Tavern: our concentration was interrupted by Captain Reid informing us all that we were setting sail again just after 6:00 pm. With the quiz over (Deb beat me again) it was a back to the cabin to freshen up and change into tidier clothes for dinner. The evening's entertainment was a change from the usual cabaret singers and featured a show by a magician. I always enjoy an act that doesn't rely on singing, and I have always had a fascination for magic, so was happy to watch this performance.

A late night drink in Andersons rounded off the day as we chatted about our adventures and just how much we had enjoyed the walk, even if it had been a little more exertive than we had planned.

+++

On Sunday the 25th July 2010 we woke up and looked out of our balcony on *Arcadia* to see that we were at anchor just off the port of Santa Margherita. This was our third visit to this port, and like the majority of the days we have spent in the Mediterranean the sun was shining with a promise of a very hot day to come.

Captain Ian Walters made his early morning announcement while we were at breakfast to say that we had arrived and then handed over to his deputy to give the details of the day's tendering operations. Our plans were to go ashore and catch a ferry for the 20-minute ride around the coast to Portofino.

We relaxed and enjoyed the views until the organised tours had left, then we gathered up our bits and pieces and went to the Piano Bar to collect tickets for the tender. There was quite a crowd waiting by the time we got our tickets and several of the waiting passengers were suffering frayed tempers. I couldn't understand the problem with these people who seemed to think that there should not be any waiting. It was no more than fifteen or twenty minutes and then we were away across the bay to the little harbour. From there we quickly found the ferry to Portofino, bought our tickets and jumped aboard with a wonderful view from the top deck.

The nearby beach was already packed with bathers and sun-worshippers and it wasn't 10:00 am yet, but the water did look inviting. Soon the ferry honked its horn and we were away for the scenic ride around the beautiful coastline.

In Portofino our plans were to retrace our route from our first visit in 2001 and see if we recognised any of it. At the top of the pebbled landing area we turned left up the hill and came to the church of St George. Across the pathway from the church is a superb view down onto the harbour area with its coloured buildings and green hills behind, and a number of villas almost hidden away amongst the vegetation. Every now and then a horn tooted breaking the near-silence to announce the arrival of the bus from Santa Margherita. The little port was pretty, but it was also a haven for the rich and famous, and the tranquil deep blue water was littered with large boats and yachts. A few fishing boats bobbed about between the gleaming white hulls of the classier vessels.

We wandered along the cliff path looking at the houses hidden away behind tall hedges, and getting an occasional view between the trees to the sea below. There was even a wonderful sighting of *Arcadia* in the distance. Our walk took us as far as a magnificent building known as the Brown Castle on one of the highest points around the port, and that was far enough. It was time to retrace our steps down to the harbour area for a bit of window shopping and an ice-cream.

One thing we did notice that was totally different to our previous visit was the sight of a row of six-foot-high purple meerkats on the top of stone pillars surrounded by equally colourful flowers. I am not sure this was a sight totally in tune with the atmosphere of this very, very, special little place.

Hot and tired, and yes just a little hungry maybe, we caught the ferry back to Santa Margherita and then the tender back to *Arcadia*. It had been a short but extremely sweet morning and I felt pleased to have gone back to see Portofino again.

At 5:30 pm our relaxation was disturbed by Captain Walters coming on the PA system to announce it was time to set sail again. He gave us details of the journey to our next port, and reported that the anchors had been weighed (strange term). Very soon we were sailing away from Santa Margherita on a delightful sunny evening.

If we had been a little more adventurous we could have joined one of the other tours and seen more. We could have gone on a day's exploration of Genoa, or a little closer the town of Sestri Levante. These involved a fair bit of walking so a less energetic option was a more panoramic tour around the Ligurian region or even a boat trip around the coastline.

We were more than happy with what we did, but if we ever come back to this part of Italy, perhaps we will explore a little more.

Livorno

Perhaps 100 miles south of Santa Margherita is the port of Livorno, and we arrived there aboard *Oriana* on Saturday 16th July 2005. As a cruise holiday destination the port is not the main event: this is where passengers take coaches to the beautiful cities of Florence or Pisa.

Captain Mike Carr had *Oriana* tied to the dockside before 8:00 in the morning in time to offload hundreds of passengers to find their guides and board the coaches for their various tours. We had decided not to split our time between two places and concentrate our day on Florence. Deb and I were off the ship just after 9:00 am with little stickers to show we were on Tour B, titled as an Introduction to Florence.

It was over an hour's drive from Livorno, which allowed the guide plenty of time to talk about Italy in general, and Livorno and Florence in particular, as well as giving us an overview of what we would be seeing during the day. Many of us took the chance to just look at the passing countryside, and rest our eyes after an early rise for breakfast.

On the way to Florence there was a moment of excitement, as those on the right-hand side of the coach caught a glimpse of Pisa in the distance, and the rather obvious leaning tower. At least we saw it even if we didn't get the chance to be photographed in that famous pose seemingly holding up the tower.

...never mind, we saw many examples of it from the other passengers

Once we arrived in the wonderful city of Florence (Firenza to Italians) we said goodbye to our driver and set off for a few hours exploration on foot. Our drop-off point was the Santa Croce Piazza, a square surrounded by three and four-storey buildings painted in the typical Mediterranean pastel colours.

At one end of the square is the Franciscan style church, the Basilica of Saint Croce, where Galileo, Michelangelo and Machiavelli are buried. We spent a moment looking at the three sets of imposing carved wooden doors surrounded by friezes. We couldn't go inside, but we did look around the gardens and cloisters area at the rear. Back in the square our guide pointed out signs and stains on the walls showing the height that floodwater reached in 1966.

Tour Group B now walked through the Triumphal Arch towards the Piazza Republica. This square features the Column of Abundance in the centre, which marks the spot where Roman dignitaries used to speak to their people. Nowadays it is a commercial area with shops, restaurants and cafés making it a lovely place for visitors and locals to sit and relax.

Onwards again and our next stop was at the Piazza della Signoria, with the Palazzo Vecchio that looks like a church with a tall bell tower. More importantly, this square features fountains and a replica of the famous Statue of David. Even this replica attracts hundreds of tourists each day who haven't the time to queue up and see the original at the Galleria dell'Accademia. Well I have to say that the replica was rather inspirational, and at least I now know what the real statue looks like.

Also on one side of the same square was what looked like a barn but it was full of statues and bits of monuments. It looked like it was a storage area for items of art that could not be put on display anywhere else. I had no idea who the sculptors were and if anything was valuable but the sight of all these marble objects simply stored in an open warehouse was quite unbelievable.

The guide gave us an hour's free time to explore by ourselves (and probably to give him time for his lunch and a well-earned rest). Our stomachs were suggesting we ought to find something to eat too, and after exploring the Piazza della Signoria for a little while longer, we wandered down a side street in search of a café.

There were several places with windows full of temptations, but after considering a few, a smiling face in one of the cafes was enough to get us to go in. Looking at the glass display cabinet full of food, it was difficult to choose what to eat, but with assistance from the owner we eventually decided on a cheese and ham Panini and a glass of cola. Now, back in Britain we had in the past eaten many Paninis, but in that café they were beyond delicious with better quality bread and the most fantastic ham and cheese. It was so good that we went back to the counter and chose one of their glorious cakes to eat as well. When we left, the owner and the waitress smiled and waved us off as we thanked them for a terrific lunch.

We still had a little while before meeting up with the guide again, and our exploration took us to the Uffizi Palace – well, along the outside of it anyway. This area is like an open-air quadrangle with pillared covered walkways where a busker was playing a guitar and gathering quite a crowd listening to his flawless classical music. This was one of the few times I have ever been tempted to buy a CD from a busker.

There were also several people painting the scene or selling their artwork to the crowds of tourists walking up and down. We were not interested in buying anything that serious and instead we looked at the life-size statues of Italian artists and scientists that were displayed in alcoves set into the walls of the palace.

...the artwork on display in this city is simply stunning

Lunch time over we met up with the group and our guide again. We walked on down some more streets and came to the River Arno at the point where it is crossed by the famous Ponte Vecchio.

As we approached this renowned 14th Century river crossing, it initially looked little more than a bridge that had houses built into its side. My views changed however as we started to go over it and discovered it was lined with shops on both sides selling all kinds of high-end goods, with an abundance of gold and silver jewellery. This was a moment of experiencing a spectacle rather than buying anything...especially at the somewhat inflated prices for already expensive items. The bridge was a surprise and really quite charming and special.

It seems that Florence has more than its fair share of architecture and artistic gems, and this day was turning into a pleasure overdose.

Several photographs and cries of "**wow**" later, our guide convinced us there was still more to see, so it was back into the narrow streets again. This time we were taken to see the area around the Cathedral of Florence. Yes here was another building that has an A-star for architectural beauty, combined with a further top grade for artistic presentation. The main entrance door was wonderful but the façade around it was covered in sculptured windows and alcoves containing more statues. As we looked up there was a sensational tall

Campanile and to the side of it a magnificent dome, or Cupola. The crowds were queuing just to get close enough to look at the cathedral, and we were coaxed away by our guide so that others could enjoy the view. This was not a problem as across the road was the Baptistery of San Giovanni, giving us another building to drool over, especially its bronze doors with panels depicting scenes from the Old Testament.

Well, that was the final part of our tour and our heads were swimming as we walked back to the Piazza della Signoria to wait for our coach to arrive. This gave us a final chance to look at the Statue of David, as well as Verrochio's Dolphin Boy Fountain, while we cooled our throats with an ice-cream.

Back on the coach our guide answered questions about our visit for a while, until he sensed the silence meant we were having a rest. Someone was alert enough to point out that we were passing Pisa again, giving those who missed it in the morning a chance to grab a very distant photograph.

We have never been back to Florence but I am sure that one day we will spot a cruise on the right ship at the right time and we will have another chance to explore it.

This had been an exhausting day, but also so exhilarating to have had the chance to visit a beautiful city that boasts so much art and so many historical buildings.

Back on board *Oriana* that evening there was a deck party, but many people took the opportunity of having an early night, as the next day would be another long one with a visit to Rome for most of the passengers.

Civitavecchia

Where on earth (I hear some of you say) is Civitavecchia, and how do you pronounce it?

Well, it's quite a large port about half way between Livorno and Naples...but more importantly it's the port that serves as the gateway between the sea and Rome which is some 45 miles inland. To pronounce the name some basic Italian will help. Usually a '*C*' is pronounced as a 'ch' whilst a '*Ch*' is a 'k'. The rest of the name is reasonably straight forward...

>...*Chivitavekia*...and it means **old city**

Well we arrived at this port on Saturday 24th August 2002 aboard the beautiful *Oriana* captained by Hamish Reid. Just before 8:00 in the morning we were moored alongside and the majority of the passengers had already finished their breakfast in time for an early getaway to the capital of Italy.

We heard later that there was hardly anyone left on board *Oriana* that day.

Like many people we had a tour booked: an all-day trip to Rome with a guided tour of the highlights as well as some free time to explore. With pretty stickers on our chests we quickly made our way down to the quayside and got on our coach for a drive on busy roads to the city.

Our guide gave us the usual chat about the landmarks we were passing and what we would be seeing and doing in Rome. She gave us quite a lecture about being aware of pickpockets who cause mayhem in the city with tourists distracted by the sights we would be seeing. The warning was especially aimed at the men as many of the pickpocket gangs use pretty young girls to put you off your guard.

The traffic increased in volume as we got closer to the city, and it was mid-morning by the time we got off our coach to be greeted by the heat of a wonderful sunny day. The drop off point was just a short walk from the first of the day's highlights at the Trevi Fountain. This was not what we were expecting as I, and many others, thought it would be a large ornate circular fountain rather than a construction built against a background wall. It was still amazing with an ornate, and huge marble façade almost 50 metres wide and over 25 metres high.

This magnificent monument has several statues in the central arch, and to its sides in what look like false windows between pillars, and at the very top is another group of sculptures with angels surveying the scene below. In front of the façade is an apparently random rockery, and various sculptures, with water trickling down through the marble treats before falling over the ledge into the main pool. This pool is semi-circular and the same width as the façade and almost as far forwards.

It has a low wall all the way around where many of the hundreds of visitors sat and performed the custom of throwing coins over their shoulder into the fountain's water.

It is said that if you throw three coins into the Trevi fountain you will return to Rome one day.

Of course Deb duly took her position on the wall and threw three coins over her shoulder with a wish to hope to return.

...yes alright, I did it too!

The noise of the water, and the babble of the crowds, mix with the wonderful scene and make this a sensational first image we had of Rome.

It was time now to take a stroll through some backstreets until we arrived at the next "**wow**" moment at the area known as the Forum where without moving more than 50 metres you can see a number of historical and beautiful sights. The first that we were directed to look at was the building known as the Monumento Vittoria Emanuelle II. This Emanuelle II was apparently the first king of Italy, but Deb was not too sure what happened to Emanuelle I!   His personal building is at the top of some steps and has winged charioteers on either side of its roof. Known locally as *The Wedding Cake* it also houses the Tomb of the Unknown Warrior.

By now my video camera was working flat out capturing memories, while Deb was just about to start the second roll of film in her still camera. I wasn't really listening intently to our guide even though she was giving a marvellous description of all the buildings around us. However I did pay attention when she pointed out another impressive building which was the Imperial Palace where Benito Mussolini stood on a balcony and urged his people to follow his ideology.

Across the road were the ruins of the Forum of Augustus. This enormous space with the Temple of Mars at one end was a meeting place where the emperor spoke to his people. This vast area now has remnants of the walls plus rows of broken or fallen pillars that probably held the statues of famous soldiers and dignitaries. I was still not concentrating on our guide's commentary and really couldn't make a lot of sense of this area, but I realised I was looking at an area that was an architectural gem and real history.

Although the details are a little hazy, we did stop at some point and had a light meal in a hotel overlooking a square. It was probably Italian bread, Parma ham, cheeses and wine but maybe that is how I like to remember it. One very important part of this lunchtime snack was the chance to get out of the sun for a while as well as a moment to sit down.

This tour was quite intense and we were soon walking up a little hill and then along a road where there was little shade from the blazing sunshine, and the temperatures were approaching 30°C by now. Not listening to the guide again, I was unsure of where we were going until I spotted a shape in the distance that I recognised as the Coliseum. In such a short time I had already seen so many amazing sights and here was another that I had seen in books and on the television, but now it was actually standing in front of me.

I am sure most of you have seen pictures of this iconic piece of history but believe me it is even more impressive up close. Its sheer size can't be imagined until you look at the arches and see people who appear tiny. We were unfortunately not able to go inside as our time was short and queues to enter were enormous, but we did have time to wander around and get a feeling for the place.

There were men dressed up as centurions tempting the visitors to take photos (at a cost), and everywhere you looked there were salesmen trying to sell us watches and sunglasses, but most of us avoided them all. Then without warning the sky clouded over and we had a shower of rain. It wasn't too bad and hardly a disturbance, but we were amazed that suddenly those same salesmen were now offering umbrellas, but they were still not very successful.

On our way back from the Coliseum back the way that we had come, we stopped in another vast space (I think it was the Forum of Rome) with more ruins. This was once where the Basilica Aemilia stood although just broken pillars and slabs of marble remain. In the same location we also saw the remains of the Temple of Venus Genetrix, the Temple of Antonius and Faustina, and the Arch of Septimus.

I think you need a lot more time than we had to make sense of all the various temples and arches with their pillars and tonnes of marble.

It was time now for the finale of our day in Rome - St Peter's Square and the Vatican.

We retraced our steps before turning a corner to reveal St Peter's Square. It is stunning, enormous, and very busy with tourists from all over the world. The square is actually a circle with a simple Egyptian obelisk pillar in its centre that has a cross on the top. Like many others we approached the square along the Via della Conciliazione which is a straight road about 500 metres long. Initially as you walk down the road you see the dome and façade of the Basilica of St Peter, but then the vastness of the square hits you. This square, plus the basilica (church) and the neighbouring buildings, are not a part of Italy as they belong to the State that is known as Vatican City.

Now I initially said it was circular, but to be precise the central area of the 100 acre site is created as a keyhole shape with the church at the narrower end. Around the circle, where thousands of visitors congregate each Sunday to see the Pope, are two colonnades. They are constructed with multiple rows of pillars and allow shelter from the rain (or the sun) as well as creating a fantastic architectural spectacle. On the roof of those colonnades are a series of statues. Behind those colonnades are more buildings including offices and the private apartments of the Pope. Underground there is even a coach park where we would eventually be going to find our ride back to the ship.

Most of our group were now staring open-mouthed at the size of the vast square, the beautiful colonnades around it, and the buildings with the balcony where the Pope addresses the faithful. But the most striking sight was the huge pillared façade and dome of the Basilica of St Peter that was dominating our view. There are steps leading up to the main entrance with officers of the Swiss Guard in their colourful uniforms protecting the church with their state-of-the-art pikestaffs. Above the front of the building there is a row of statues depicting various saints and angels and they are over 20 feet high but the sheer size of the Basilica makes them appear small.

As we walked closer to the entrance, the dome that had been so dominant disappeared from view as the façade towered above us. There were hundreds of visitors staring at the scene but hundreds more queuing up to one side for their look around the church. Fortunately our tour group had pre-paid tickets, and we were able to jump most of the queue and were very soon shuffling along to the side entrance.

Once inside, the heat of the sun was gone, and the outside noise subsided. The Basilica is enormous. The main body of the church is 46 metres high and 186 metres long, with a further 30 metres for the porch area. The stupendous dome is 46 metres in diameter and extends to 136 metres above the floor. The Basilica of St Peter is one of the largest churches in the world and you cannot fail to be amazed by its size and beauty. The guide pointed out brass strips on the floor as we walked up the main body of the church. Each one marks the length of the different major churches around the world just to show how much bigger this one is. It dwarfs Westminster Abbey and is longer than St Pauls by several metres.

We had perhaps 30 minutes inside that allowed us time to look at so much while our guide gave a wonderful description and explanation of what we were seeing. There are small chapel areas to the sides every now and then and they often had groups of people praying or quietly chanting. After passing by a couple of these groups I put down my camera. I am not a believer and I felt I was invading a very special place for these people from all over the world who had made a pilgrimage to be here. For the rest of those amazing minutes in the Basilica I looked and enjoyed the architecture, the artwork, the statues, the religious treasures and relics, the little chapels, and the wonderful dome above with its painted ceiling. Even though I felt uncomfortable about being in there, I was absorbed by its magnificence and understood why so many people feel drawn to it.

Our tour of the Basilica was over and we had a little time to take a last look around the square. We went in search of a souvenir in the shops nearby, and although it shouldn't have been a surprise, we were disappointed by the choice. Almost everything was religious, be it pictures of popes, or statuettes of the Madonna or the various saints.

It was time for us to go down to the coach park and meet up with the rest of the group and our guide. The coach trip back was quite subdued as it was nearly 5:00 in the afternoon and we had been away from *Oriana* for over 8 hours. Our lovely guide tried to keep us occupied, but like on so many long trips we have been on over the years, a lot of us just wanted to close our eyes and remember a fantastic day.

By the time we were back on the ship the engines were revving up for a quick getaway. There was just long enough to dump our purchases from the day and have a very quick shower before it was dinnertime.

This had been a very special day with a tour that allowed us to see so many wonderful sights but we realised there was much more to see in the city of Rome. We knew that we had to come back and spend a more relaxed day in Rome and explore a few places in greater detail.

+++

Well it took us three years but those *three little coins in the fountain* worked and we did go back to Rome.

It was Sunday 17th July 2005 and we were on board *Oriana*. We had been in Florence the day before and we were already exhausted, but if Rome is available then it is hard to miss the opportunity of visiting.

It was another early morning, and after a hearty breakfast to keep us going we were climbing onto a coach for a trip known as *Rome on Your Own*. This means that we had a coach ride to the city with a guide to point out a few facts and instructions on the way. We then had about six hours to do our own thing in the city before meeting up again late in the afternoon for the return journey.

It was another stunning day with blue skies and temperatures set to rise into the mid-20°s so we were prepared with bottles of water, sun-screen and hats.

Our drop-off point was the coach park below the Vatican area, and having been suitably warned about pickpockets we emerged into the bright sunshine of St Peter's Square to begin our adventure.

The day was going to be far more relaxed than being on an organised tour, as we could spend time getting our bearings and just savouring the views in the Square. It wasn't as busy as the last time we visited, but there were long queues of people waiting to get inside the Basilica. Pope John Paul II had died three months before and the world's Catholics wanted to come and see his tomb. Being Sunday of course there were also worshippers and presumably a lot of people would appear in the Square later in the hopes of a glimpse of the new Pope (Benedict XVI) on his balcony. We had no intention of being around to find out, and were making the most of the Square while it was relatively deserted.

So we looked at the obelisk from all angles, then inspected the magnificent fountain designed by Bernini, before looking in awe at the statues on the columned wings around the outside, and of course the amazing Basilica façade. There were a few minutes simply sitting on the edge of the Square surveying the Pope's Palace while we decided what we would do next.

It wasn't long before we spotted the hop-on-hop-off bus stop, and we bought our tickets for a panoramic circuit of the city. These buses are found in almost every major city in the world and are a simple and effective way of seeing the majority of the tourist hot spots. We found seats on the open top deck near to the front, and sat back to enjoy a couple of hours of Roman masterpieces.

We passed through a mix of busy streets as well as seeing the architectural gems, but even the buildings of the commercial areas with the Sunday morning life was interesting. From the tourist perspective we were thrilled to see beautiful piazzas (squares) around almost every corner and they all seemed to feature fountains.

The route took us around the Forum area to remind us of the abundance of marble pillars that were built in this city so many centuries ago. There on the nearby Caelian Hill was the Wedding Cake Building with the Italian flags flying proudly at the foot of the steps leading up to it, and across the road was Mussolini's window. A couple of streets later and we were driving around the Trevi Fountain where a small army of people were lobbing coins over their shoulders into the clear sparkling water. We took our chance to get off here and get up close to it and Deb did her best to ensure we would come back yet again.

Back on our bus we continued our circuit and then had a shock as we stopped presumably at a terminus point where the driver changed. Unfortunately it was a position with nothing to look at and we were wilting in the heat of the upstairs position. After what seemed an eternity we continued knowing that our route would soon get to where we intended to have a longer stop...The Coliseum.

This time we had made our minds up to go inside and really explore this place properly.

The queues were horrendous but while we were standing in line we noticed signs advertising guided tours in various languages, but also suggesting there were no queues. The prices didn't seem excessive so we jumped from our snaking line and went to the booth for the English version of the tour. A few euros later and we were following a young Italian guide who showed off a good mastery of English, and entered the Colosseum.

It was stupendous. It was even bigger than I expected, and we made our way along the walkways around the outside, while our guide brought it to life as he explained its history. I could almost imagine the scene with thousands of Romans walking to their seats to watch the evening's entertainment. The men complaining about the hours at work, and then trying to explain an intricate rule of the evening's sport while the salesmen shouted to attract customers with their Panini and mead drinks...

...I know I'm just being a soppy dreamer

Down below was the stage area built above a labyrinth of corridors, and remains of rooms where maybe the slaves waited their turn to face the lions or inevitable death at the hands of prize-fighting centurions.

Our guide pointed out a diagram on the wall showing that the Colosseum once had a full roof covering, making this auditorium even more impressive, especially considering it is larger than most major football grounds.

After a wonderful hour in this sensational place we turned to our maps and made our way along the road to St Peter's Square again with some thoughts of going inside the Basilica. But when we got there our main consideration was to get a drink and sit down in the shade, so we abandoned the idea of going inside the church. There wasn't a great deal of time left before our departure anyway, so we looked in the shops before making our way down to the coach park in search of our air-conditioned transport.

It had been a hot, tiring, but superb day. Our cameras had recorded more memories to keep us happy when we look through the albums. But for now we sat back in the coach seats, listened to the chatter from the guide and the other excited passengers, and dozed as we made our way back to *Oriana*, and a welcoming shower.

Just after 6:00 in the evening, Captain Mike Carr opened the throttle and our floating hotel set sail again on the way to our next Italian delight. Sipping a cool glass of wine and watching the sail-away we wondered if we would be coming back again.

+++

Five years later we eventually returned to Civitavecchia sailing in early in the morning aboard *Arcadia* (current one). Captain Ian Walters had us tied up alongside by 7:30 in the morning in readiness for the mass exodus of his passengers. Most would be taking the long journey to the Eternal City but we had decided that two visits to Rome were enough (for now) and we fancied seeing something else that didn't involve a long coach ride.

Our tour was a guided look around the city of Tuscania, together with a visit to an olive farm.

Tuscania is in the region of Lazio and is quite small, with a population of less than 10,000. On a hill just away from the city centre is the old Church of St Pietro. It is a beautiful church with an ornate circular window above the main entrance and inside it is full of pillars that hold up numerous arches. It has several other buildings and towers that are partially destroyed as well as some defensive walls to wander around.

In the centre of the small city (or is it a town?) there is another church (St Maria Maggiore) which stands at the end of a little square and looks a little more modern with another circular window. You may well have noticed my lack of interest of churches so it won't surprise anyone that I didn't spend much time looking around them.

I was more impressed with a fountain in the square. It spouted water from jets in the centre of a bowl that was supported above the main collection area, where there were strange statuette figures like some grotesque sea creatures with further water jets from tubes in their mouths. Like most of the tour group we took the opportunity of having a cappuccino outside of the café that was next to the fountain.

After a gentle stroll around the city our guide ushered us back to the coach for the ride up into the hills to an Agriturismo Olive Farm. There are many of these touristic-agriculture ventures in the countryside of Italy, and they give visitors a chance to look at vineyards and olive grove farming. Of course they also give the tourists a chance to sample the crops and many people buy some of the produce as well.

Anyway we enjoyed the visit looking at the trees of different ages and seeing a demonstration of harvesting by shaking the trees to catch the ripe olives. With a guided walk through the production area we ended up sitting at tables with glasses of wine and local bread to sample the olive oil. I am only just getting into the taste of olives, and while I can at least now eat the olive itself, I find it a little overpowering to eat bread that is dipped into the oil. The idea of drinking it really makes me feel a little queasy but many of the group (including Deb) seemed happy with the idea and reported that the taste was wonderful.

I was quite happy with the bread, cheese, and olive paste, plus my glass or two of red wine.

Time was up, and one by one the group returned to the coach many with carrier bags or even boxes of the farmer's produce to take home. We hadn't bothered as a jar of olives lasts several weeks in our house and Deb is quite happy with whatever Sainsbury's has to offer.

Less than an hour later we were back on *Arcadia* with a chance to relax by the pool and plenty of loungers to choose from. The tours to Rome were not back for a couple of hours yet, and this was one of the magic moments of an almost deserted ship.

This had been a rather splendid day and we were not exhausted as on the other two visits to Civitavecchia. Perhaps if we come back, or should I say *when* we come back, the idea of visiting Rome will be more appealing again, but for now we believed we had made the best decision to bypass it this time.

As the afternoon turned to evening, the passengers returned and Captain Walters eventually made his usual speech. He always rounds off a day in a port by saying, *"Welcome back...welcome home"*. It was time to leave this busy port and after waiting for our turn, we moved away from the dockside and made our way out into the beautiful calm waters of the Mediterranean.

Naples

It was the 27th July 2001, it was my 50th birthday, and early in the morning the good ship *Arcadia* (the older version!) arrived at the port of Naples. This is a busy port and Naples is rated as the third biggest city in Italy after Rome and Milan, with a population of more than 3.5 million people. Geographically it is about a third of the way up the western coast from the southernmost tip, or 'toe' of Italy.

Although the city of Naples has a lot to look at, the majority of cruise ship passengers probably get off their ships and make their way to one or more of the very special places nearby. The city lies in the Bay of Naples (sometimes called the Gulf of Naples), where the stunning Amalfi coast arcs around to the beautiful town of Sorrento. Just a little way off the coast from Sorrento is the magical island of Capri, but perhaps you would like something a little more cultural. How about a short bus or train ride to the ruins of Herculaneum or Pompeii, with the menacing Mount Vesuvius in the distance?

Our decision on this particular cruise was a tour that took us to Sorrento for the morning. On our coach ride along the Amalfi coastline we had a stop to look at the sensational views from the cliffs out across the bay. On our arrival in Sorrento we had a walking tour followed by a superb lunch in a local hotel. There was also time to look at the shops and try out the lemon liqueur, or sniff the lemon soap, or just pick a fruit from the trees lining the sides of every street.

From Sorrento we drove back around the Bay again before stopping for a guided walk around the unbelievable ruins of Pompeii. We only had about two hours there and this was far too short to really appreciate the site but it was still an experience that I will never forget.

Pompeii is not just a pile of rocks or bits of walls, this is a city uncovered from its tomb of volcanic ash to reveal almost complete buildings that still have paintings on the walls. This was a busy city with all that you expect to find: houses, shops, places to worship, entertainment venues and even a brothel complete with pornographic graffiti to show the customers (male and female) what was on offer. There was a bakery with pots intact; you can walk along cobbled pathways with name signs, and water troughs, or visit the small amphitheatre with its banking of stoned seating. And yes, there are people mummified where they died as the cloud of dust enveloped them.

This is all history now, but minutes before Vesuvius death-cloud descended, life in Pompeii was going on as normal with families eating, shopkeepers serving customers, dogs following their masters and children playing.

I cannot describe Pompeii enough to give a true and full picture. You must to go there yourself and get the services of a really good guide (as we had) who can tell you the story of what you are seeing as you walk down streets where shops stood, or visit a villa where the rich lived, or kitchens where slaves worked until the moment they died.

And all the time, in the distance is the menacing view of Vesuvius quietly resting but which could repeat its angry game at any time.

If I could have seen this as a child in school perhaps I would have taken more interest in the subject, or treated history lessons a little more seriously. In fact if I had visited the countries I have been to on our cruises around the world, I would have understood so much more of history and geography, and life outside of the tiny micro-world that I live in.

Sorry, I've digressed into some philosophic ranting about the weakness of trying to teach children about vast amounts of facts with just text and photographs from a book or a PowerPoint presentation. It took over thirty years after my formal education was completed for me to suddenly realise the magnificence of the world with its varied and changing geography, its unending history, the architectural sensations that man has created, and the beautiful differences in culture from country to country.

Well our short trip around Pompeii was actually longer than it should have been, and by the time we eventually got back to the port in Naples our captain was chomping at the bit to set *Arcadia* free from its moorings. The ships officers don't like waiting past the official departure time, but fortunately with a tour organised by the on-board sales team, they are obliged to delay sailing.

What an absolutely superb day, and what a birthday.

To round off a truly wonderful day, Deb had even organised a birthday cake to arrive at the dinner table with the waiters singing "Happy Birthday" to me.

We had already decided that we had to come back to Naples and explore Pompeii properly as well as seeing more of the area.

+++

Our first return to Naples was in 2005 on the wonderful *Oriana*.

It was Monday 18th July and we were having breakfast as the ship tied up at her berth. Today we were going to do our own thing and having looked at all the guide books our plan was to get a taxi to the railway station and then go by train to Pompeii. We were in no rush, and we relaxed while the majority of the passengers disembarked to get on their tour coaches. When things seemed to have calmed down we gathered together our hats, drinks, and cameras as well as a liberal coating of sun-screen.

As we got off the ship we were met by a group of very vocal taxi drivers suggesting we should take one of their amazing tours. We quietly ignored their suggestions and asked for a simple ride to the railway station. Our driver set off and asked what our plans were, and we told him about our trip to Pompeii.

...bad mistake.

He turned around (while still driving) and did everything possible to convince us that he should take us and show us around.

...we kept saying no thanks.

Still turning to face the wrong way, he suggested driving us there and collecting us later, would be very much quicker than the train journey.

...we loudly said NO!

He was frightening us with his driving. It was fast, like all Italian taxi drivers, but we really wanted him to look where he was going. Eventually we arrived at the train station, and still refusing his offers, we paid him and rushed away with an instant comment to each other that we would walk back to the ship from the station later.

At the station we looked at all the posters and struggled to understand the ticket prices. We knew we wanted the Circumvesuviana line so we decided to adopt the British tourist method and ask for help at the ticket window. The lady was very nice and quickly worked out what we wanted. It was just €2.30 each for a return journey, and a train left every hour.

This was amazingly cheap.

It was not long before we were on a train which had very basic, and rattly carriages. This was not much of an issue as the ride was only about 40 minutes. The Circumvesuviana line, as the name suggests, travels back and forth from Naples, along the coast past Mount Vesuvius to Sorrento. It is a beautiful route but today we were only going part of the way. Once at the station (Pompeii Scavi) it was a short walk to the historical site, and we quickly bought entrance tickets and a guide book to start our exploration.

In the four years since our first visit, a lot of work had been done to restore more buildings but more noticeable was the amount of plants that had grown. Apparently some of the original plant seeds have grown naturally, but other plants have also been grown that are typical of the time.

One of the first things we went to see were the large and small theatres. We hadn't seen these on our first visit so this was a chance to see something completely different. There was little that had been destroyed at these theatres, and they look almost the same as many amphitheatres that we have seen around Italy. We had a leisurely look around them and perched ourselves on various levels of the banks of stone seating in order to get the best photos. By the way, it was very hot that day and these theatres give no shelter from the sun.

Nearby we found what is called the Arcade Court which is a rectangular space with pillars around it that supported a roof. At one end the roof has been restored and this gave us some shelter at last. Apparently this area is where theatre goers met up before performances and probably had a drink or two of wine that perhaps anesthetised the rear end a little in readiness for the hard seats.

From the theatres we moved to the remains of an old fabric market with marble display units and a counter flanked by pillars. The records indicate this market was called Eumachio, and probably sold the very best designer label items of the day. Another building that we had not seen before was the Basilica. Maybe not up to the size and standard of St Peter's but no doubt impressive before being flattened by the volcanic ash.

We turned now into one of the major streets (Via di Stabio) that took us by some beautiful alleyways where we spotted mosaic floors and courtyards with water features, and more pillars of course. Some of these courtyards had gardens that have been restocked with greenery and I could imagine a family enjoying an evening in their back garden with a glass of wine while watching the sun set.

By now we needed a rest, and we followed the signs to a more modern building that housed a café and toilets. After our recent visit to Florence where our lunchtime snack had been so delicious, this was a real disappointment. We chose a Panini similar to the one we'd had in Florence, but the bread was mass produced and the filling tasteless. This was such a difference and one of the few places we have visited in Italy where profit appears to be the main concern rather than quality.

Back to ancient cultural matters, and we headed to the familiar area of the Forum with its temples and the backdrop of Vesuvius reminding visitors that Pompeii may appear to be alive again, but one good cough from the volcano and it could all be destroyed once more.

Deb and I were tiring by now and we made our way towards the exit passing one of the many display areas with a few of the mummified bodies and shelf upon shelf of pottery and marble bits and pieces. The archaeologists have a job for life here, cataloguing and restoring as much as possible of this snapshot of that historic day in the year 9 AD.

We said goodbye to Pompeii and were soon on a train back towards Naples. The train was almost deserted but we felt a little uncomfortable with a man and woman holding a baby. Not the best dressed, they were walking up and down the train begging and just didn't look very friendly. The train guard was sitting near us and obviously looking out for us as he shouted something at the man and waved him away from us. This is something for the intrepid *do-it-alone* amongst you to bear in mind: the British tourist often looks out of place and many of us have little knowledge of the language. The beggars will target you, so be careful and try and stay in a crowd on journeys out of the city areas.

Back in Naples we walked towards the harbour and learnt a little about crossing busy roads. The tip is to find an older lady and follow her. The traffic screeches to a halt when an old lady walks out into the road. The mad drivers ignore everyone else, and pedestrian crossings are treated as merely a decoration on the road.

Anyway, we were back aboard *Arcadia* by late afternoon where we changed into fresh t-shirts and shorts to replace our dirty, sweaty clothes of the morning. The air conditioning and drinks from the fridge cooled and rehydrated us in time to watch our departure from Naples.

As we sailed away, Vesuvius dominated the horizon. Dormant she may be, but she will almost certainly wake up again one day and destroy the peaceful beauty of this wonderful area of Italy. We had seen enough of Pompeii to satisfy our interest, but Naples was a gateway to other delights and another return visit was still needed.

+++

We were back on Tuesday 29th July 2008. The ship this time was *Aurora* and the captain was Ian Hutley.

Today Deb and I were on an organised tour again, but this time we were boarding a hydrofoil ferry that would take us across the Bay of Naples for an all-day exploration of the island of Capri. It was misty as we slowly left the Naples harbour, but the hydrofoil quickly gained speed and after a few minutes the sun started to burn off the mist and we began to see glimpses of the island.

The ride across the bay was smooth and the boat was quite comfortable filled with everyday passengers as well as the P&O tour groups. As we approached the steep cliffs of Capri our boat slowed and our level of excitement rose.

By 10:00 am we had arrived at the Porto Marina Grande (Large Port) and our guide gathered us together to explain the plan for the day. The tour started with a mini-bus ride up the steep and winding hills of the island to the town of Anacapri. It was a beautiful place, where seemingly every wall and roof was covered in flowers.

Our guide pointed out a large souvenir shop and craft factory where we could look around, and use the toilet if needed. The shop was pleasant but they didn't sell us very much.

Outside the guide gave us some time to look at other nearby shops, or to have a cup of coffee, but he also suggested a ride on the cable car to the top of the island at Monte Solaro.

...I am terrified of both heights and cable cars!!

Deb laughed, and the guide said I shouldn't be afraid as it never rises more than a couple of metres above the ground. So I relented and jumped onto one of the single-seat chairs with a bar in front of me and a pole to hold onto. My legs dangled without support and I clung to my camera and the pole and looked firmly ahead to where Deb was looking around at the horror on my face.

The guide had lied, and for most of the ride we were tens of metres off the ground and at each support tower I stopped breathing as the chair rumbled over the metal work.

At the top I have to admit my fear was worth facing. We had stunning views hundreds of feet down over the rocky cliffs and forests to the whitewashed houses and the deep blue of the sea beyond. From one vantage point the Faraglioni Rocks were visible, looking a little like the Needles Rocks off the Isle of Wight. A delightful treat from up there was the sight of ferries looking hardly any bigger than toys leaving a white wake behind them. The white frothy disturbed water looked similar to vapour trails from aeroplanes. And of course in the distance we could see Vesuvius dominating the skyline of the Amalfi coastline.

We couldn't stay long, and there wasn't enough time for me to go down the steps, so I had to get back on the cable car for the equally terrifying ride back down.

Yes alright, I did enjoy the views, and I was still alive.

The mini-buses appeared and we got back inside them for the ride back down to town of Capri. This was a lovely ride as our driver put on a tape of Dean Martin singing "Que Sera Sera", "Volare" and "That's Amore". We sang along as the bus swayed around the hairpin bends of the steep roads. We were all such happy people.

It was lunchtime and all the P&O groups assembled at the Ristorante La Pigna for a lovely meal of Italian food, with enough British options to satisfy the picky Brits. And the glass of two of wine also kept our spirits up on this wonderful island.

After lunch our guide took us for a walk to the Gardens of Augustus where we strolled along pathways in the shade of the tree canopy among the lush bushes and glorious flowers. The shade gave a little respite from the sun and we needed it as temperatures were as hot as I have known it anywhere. There was some free time in the gardens and I found a path to a cliff with more photogenic views of the Marina Grande and Marina Piccola (Large and Small harbours) as well as those Faraglioni Rocks again, but not from so high up as before. At one point there was an amazing view of a pedestrian-only pathway winding its way up the sheer face of the cliff from the small harbour to the gardens. It appeared to be a very difficult walk.

With our look at the gardens over the guide took us along the streets of the town and showed us where we would have to assemble again for the boat ride back to Naples. We had a couple of hours to wander around looking at the shops, but it was so hot that we stopped in a Gelateria (ice-cream shop) where we sat under a parasol licking rapidly-melting cones.

For the rest of our time on the island we gazed into designer shop windows and realised that Capri is for the rich and there was little for us to buy except in the smaller souvenir outlets tucked away in the backstreets. It was extremely hot and shade was at a premium, but we were even gently moved on by the shopkeepers if we spent too long under shop awnings.

We had thoroughly enjoyed our day, but we were actually very glad when it was time to meet up with the guide and get back on the hydrofoil.

Back in Naples there was a short walk from the ferry to the cruise terminal and our guide did his best to tell us about the delights of Naples that so few cruise passengers ever bother to discover. Most of us were not listening to him as we were desperate to get back into our air conditioned cabins for a cold drink and a refreshing shower. Our tour was quite late getting back, and as soon as we had passed through the check-in security scanners, the gangplank was hauled in and Captain Hutley sounded Aurora's hooter to bid farewell to Naples, and we returned to sea.

There was a sail-away party out on deck but we were too tired and drained by the heat for that, and rested for the short time until our sitting for dinner was announced. Later in the evening we enjoyed one of my favourite shows from the Headliners with a tribute to the group Queen. A couple of glasses of wine topped off a superb day.

That was the last time we have been to Naples, but it remains on our wish list for a return one day. There is still the Ruins of Herculaneum to look at, and I would like to go back to Sorrento as well as perhaps looking around Naples itself.

This is certainly a fantastic port with plenty to go and see to keep even the pickiest of passengers happy.

The Italian Islands

Having looked at the major ports of the western Italian coastline, it's time to turn our attention to a few of the islands that cruise ships visit. As we have just looked at Naples near the southern tip of the country, the obvious first island to look at is Sicily, which looks like a deflated ball on the toe of Italy's boot.

+++

Sicily

The island of Sicily is the point that divides the Mediterranean Sea into its Western and Eastern Basins, so perhaps not strictly in the area I am covering, but it would be a pity to ignore it so here goes.

Sicily is the biggest island in the Mediterranean Sea, with an area of just under 10,000 square miles. As a comparison, Wales is around 8,000 square miles. The island is separated from Italy's mainland by a narrow stretch of water known as the Straits of Messina which is only two miles across at its narrowest point.

The island is shaped as a rough triangle and at its widest it is roughly 140 miles west to east and about 100 miles north to south. Its population is approximately five million, which is about two million people more than Wales. It has many beautiful beaches around its coast, and inland there are mountains and the ever-present threat from Mount Etna. This volcano still regularly reminds Sicily's inhabitants of its danger, with coughs and belches of steam, dust, sparks, and now and then a bit of lava as well.

The capital city, Palermo, is in the north-west of the island and is the major population centre with over 600,000 people. Catania is on the eastern coast and has some 290,000 people and Messina at the north-east is a little less populated with about 240,000 people.

+++

We have visited the island three times on our cruises: twice calling at Messina and once at Catania.

On Saturday 28th June 2003 we sailed into the port of Messina aboard *Adonia* (the previous one) for our first-ever visit to the island of Sicily. Messina is just about the closest point to the mainland coast of Italy across the Straits. As you sail into the harbour there is a statue of the Virgin Mary on the top of a pillar welcoming you. It has an inscription – 'Vos et ipsam civitatem benedicimus', meaning 'We bless you and your city'.

Adonia was bringing us back from a busy couple of days in Dubrovnik and Venice and we decided not to have an organised tour that day. Instead we strolled around the city, and enjoyed the views. It was difficult to miss the Cathedral which stands on the Piazza del Duomo, or Cathedral Square. We didn't venture inside the cathedral but were more interested in the external features of this Norman building, with its bell tower to the side which apparently holds the biggest astronomic clock in the world. In the square stands the Orion Fountain (created by Giovanni Angelo Montorsoli) which is a typical Italian masterpiece of marble with figures of gods around it. Nearby stands the baroque column of the Virgin Mary by Giuseppe Buceti. There were plenty of photographic opportunities here.

We also found some shops and rooted out an ice-cream but that was enough for us so we wandered back towards our ship to relax for the rest of the day.

+++

We were back in Messina on the wonderful *Arcadia* (the present one) on Monday 16th July 2007. This time we chose to go on a morning tour to the beautiful little town of Taormina.

After a pleasant ride south along the coastal road we arrived at Taormina and got out of the coach and discovered it was yet another hot day. Although it only has a population of some 11,000 people, and appears relatively small, it seems Taormina is actually a city. There is a superb beach, but we spent much of our time up the hill above the coast in the old town (or city) area.

Our guide took us through an arch in a surviving section of the city wall to start our walking tour through the narrow streets. It was very peaceful, and we soaked up the atmosphere whilst looking at the local Sicilian architecture. Like almost everywhere we visit there were fountains in squares and of course the Cathedral on the edge of another Piazza del Duomo.

There was a chance to briefly look at the Old Monastery and its exhibition of puppets of all kinds of figures. The town is renowned for these intricate metre tall puppets, and I presume they come out and get paraded around the streets on festival days.

Our walk continued out onto the hillside to visit the remains of a Greek open-air theatre with a view of Mount Etna not far away on the horizon. The amphitheatre was typical of so many that we have seen, but they always fascinate me and make me climb up the top of the stone seating to look at the stage area below. This one was rather special as behind the stage was the remains of a couple of arches through which we had superb views of Bay of Taormina and Mount Etna.

We had a few minutes to wander around the theatre and found some cactus plants on the edge of the seating area that were so large that people have scratched graffiti into the leaves. It is the same the whole world over: *Kilroys* of all nations telling us that they were here, and youngsters declaring their love for someone.

Before we left, our guide pointed out a quite startling sight some distance away at the top of the hill. There, virtually clinging to the hilltop, was the small village of Castelmola. At this distance we could make out the red-tiled roofs of the stone buildings and a tall white cross that must be visible miles away.

Our morning in Taormina had been short but wonderful.

+++

In 2011 we were on *Aurora* on our way out to Venice and on 27th May we stopped off at Sicily visiting the port of Catania.

This was our third stop in Sicily but our first time at Catania. After a pleasant tour around Taormina last time, we decided to take another organised trip out that started with a visit to the city of Zafferana. It's a few miles north of our dock, and is a hillside town in the shadow of the island's infamous Mount Etna which was gently smoking as it snoozed a few miles away. The city is very small with a population of around 10,000 people, and consists mainly of narrow streets between rows of architecturally stunning houses. Some have the country's flag proudly draped over their balconies, but it's just as likely to see washing drying there.

After a few minutes' walk with our guide describing the beautiful scene around us, we turned a corner to find the cathedral sitting on one side of a stunning square. As well as being dominated by the cathedral with beautiful bronze doors, the square also had the extra treat of an ornate town hall on another side. Opposite this building there were steps leading down to a garden area with places to sit and enjoy the sun as well giving our cameras a chance to capture a picture of yet another superb fountain.

The cathedral entrance is up a number of steps with mosaic patterns in the stone. I don't know if it is always the case, but the steps had rows of pots on either side full of flowering shrubs and small bushes to brighten it up. The town hall has steps as well, but these were plain white marble with statues guarding the approach to the flag-bedecked entrance.

After looking around Zafferana we were driven into the countryside and stopped at a site where the lava flow from Etna's 1992 eruption came to a halt. It is quite stunning to see the destruction in the distance with buildings destroyed and the ground obliterated. A house stands untouched just a few metres in front of the line of lava, and the relieved local people built a monument to give thanks that the flow of destruction stopped. This monument obviously gets regular attention with an abundance of flowers around it.

When everyone had explored the rocky landscape we returned to our coach and drove further up into the hills to the main attraction of the tour at the Vivera Vineyard

This was established quite recently, and the family runs an organic farm to produce the grape vines and then create their wine.

It was quite fascinating to see what looked like quite barren volcanic rock that had been broken down into soil where vines were growing. Our first view was of young plants that looked very vulnerable, but in a field next to them rows of mature plants were well established and flourishing.

From the vines we had a tour around the manufacturing area with the daughter of the family eagerly showing what the family had created as a business. We were some of the first tourists to visit the farm and the enthusiasm was very apparent. Past huge storage areas and through halls of stainless steel vats we finally arrived at the bottle packing room where a number of workers were finishing the process before the wine was sent off all over Europe.

We showed as much enthusiasm as possible, and this was rewarded when we arrived in a large room with tables laid out with local bread, cheese, and olives, alongside glasses that were being filled with the wine for us to taste. The next hour was extremely enjoyable with the family members chatting to us as we ate and drank. A number of the groups bought some of the wine, and most of us left happy, with a warm alcoholic glow in our tums.

Our coach eventually returned our very chatty group to the ship after a very interesting morning's tour with some wonderful memories of Zafferana, and the vineyard.

Mount Etna plays a major part in the life of Sicily, especially as it has minor eruptions on a regular basis. Hence tours to see the volcano are very popular, although they can be unpredictable if Etna is in one of its more active moments.

A number of tours go up the slopes of the volcano and allow passengers to get a view of the steaming crater. They can also see the recent evidence of ash, rocks and lava that has been released onto the slopes above villages that have such a precarious existence.

We have never been on one of these tours but possibly in the future, if we get to Sicily again, this could be an interesting morning out.

Sardinia

Sardinia is the second largest of the Italian islands, in fact it is the second largest Mediterranean island. Its nearest neighbour is the French island of Corsica just over 7 miles to the north, with the Italian mainland some 120 miles to the east, and North Africa a similar distance to the south. Sardinia is a crude rectangular shape, about 150 miles north to south and some 50 miles west to east, and has a population of around 1.6 million.

Our first visit was on Thursday 26th July 2001 on board *Arcadia* (yes the previous one) with Captain Hamish Reid. The island may be quite large but the ports are small, so Arcadia was anchored a little way offshore, close to Palau and also near the tiny island of La Maddalena.

Although tours were available we took the simple option of a tender ride into Palau and a ferry from there to La Maddalena. It was a beautiful trip across to the island on the ferry-come-pleasure boat, where we sat up on the top deck to get some superb views. One special treat was being able to photograph *Arcadia* from the water as a wonderful memory of this ship.

La Maddalena is one of a number of small islands making up the archipelago of the same name. As we made our way to the port on the biggest island we passed smaller islands, such as San Stefano, Caprera, and a tiny pimple on the sea called Chiesa. The port and town of La Maddalena is a sleepy one with pastel-coloured buildings and palm trees all over the place. We had looked in the guide books to see what the island offered, and decided that nothing really stood out as somewhere to visit, so this was a morning to have a stroll and stretch our legs. This cruise was a busy one with several major ports, and today was a day to recharge our batteries.

There are many days on a cruise when we have no urge to explore a port beyond a gentle walk and just getting a feeling for a place. That day we didn't even go beyond the Piazza Umberto which is a paved square dotted with the palm trees. There are shops and cafés nearby, and after looking in a few shop windows we chose a café to sit and have a wonderful cappuccino. The town seemed almost deserted, so perhaps it hadn't been identified as a holiday resort at the time we were there. By now it could be a noisy and overcrowded resort, and totally commercialised like so many of the beautiful islands and seaside towns around the Mediterranean.

Anyway, after our coffee we were quite satisfied with our morning out and made our way back to the harbour for the return to Palau again. The journey back was just as good as previously, with gentle seas that we could hear slapping against the hull over the noise of the engines. To one side of us there was a little flotilla of tiny yachts, presumable a training school for the youngsters, and looking the other way was our beautiful white floating home.

Less than three hours from when we left *Arcadia* after breakfast, we were back on board again. It had been a very nice morning, but we had seen and done enough. For lunch we sat at a table out on the deck at the stern of the ship with a salad from the buffet. There was hardly a cloud in the sky and the sun was shining down on the calm deep blue sea as we chatted and glanced around us at some sensational views of Palau and La Maddalena. This was a wonderful moment that can often be experienced on a cruise. In the afternoon we took part in serious sun-worship until it became too hot and we retreated to the shaded side on the Promenade deck.

...what a life!!

+++

Monday 23rd June 2003 and we had arrived at the port of Cagliari in Sardinia. Our ship was *Adonia* (previous one) and was captained by Rory Smith. You probably already suspect that we didn't have a tour booked, and you would be correct. This cruise was heading towards Venice and we were saving our tour budget for the Adriatic ports, so our plans today were to have a walk around the city.

Cagliari (pronounced with a silent 'g') is the capital of the island of Sardinia, and is positioned near the southern end of the island. It has a population of a little over 150,000.

We had been to the port talk for this city and Deb stayed awake long enough to discover that it has a Roman Amphitheatre so that was our target destination along with looking for a souvenir and an ice-cream.

As usual we had our breakfast early in the Pavilion buffet while the ship was docking, and knowing that it would be hot again we were ready to get off by 9:00 am. Having been caught out by unexpected heat in the past, we went prepared with drinks and sun hats and the usual application of sun cream.

The city is pretty, and architecturally stunning with lots of beautiful buildings, tonnes of marble, and beautiful paved walkways. As we wandered through the streets we came to a picturesque square where we sat and relaxed. Our bench was in the shade and it was cool enough to sit and watch the Italians going about their daily business, and many of them were openly laughing at cruise ship tourists gazing at maps and pointing in seemingly random directions at street names.

Refreshed again, we consulted our own map and headed off up a hill towards the amphitheatre. We were hoping to have a few minutes looking at some history, and it wasn't long before we arrived at the entrance.

Our plans were not to be successful as the gates were closed. We struggled to understand the signs at the entrance, but deciphered enough to know that it was not open to the public today. We later found out that it was closed while they prepared the venue for a stage-show. The site of the amphitheatre was surrounded by quite a tall hedge but we managed to climb it enough to get a glimpse of this Roman masterpiece. Workmen were building a stage and erecting lighting and audio systems, but we could just about make out the slope of the hillside with its stunning 1800-year-old limestone seating.

Disappointed but not despondent, we enjoyed some wonderful views from the top of the hill before retracing our route back to the city shopping area. Here we found something to bring home to remind us of the day, together with a bottle of cola to keep in the cabin fridge for the hot days to come...and yes we had an ice-cream!

That was enough of Cagliari to satisfy our curiosity, especially as it was really hot and we were wilting. It was time to get out of the sun, and we were also beginning to feel peckish, so having been away from food for a couple of hours, we strolled back to *Adonia* for a spot of lunch. We'd had our fill of exploring for the day, so we made the most of our wonderful ship for the afternoon before Captain Smith hooted farewell and set sail again.

+++

We were back in Cagliari again on Tuesday 19th July 2005. This time our floating home was the beautiful *Oriana,* captained by Mike Carr.

You might be a bit shocked by this, but having already had a busy cruise, and because of the disappointment on our previous visit, we didn't even leave the ship and just had a quiet day on board.

"How could you", I hear you say. Well we enjoy all aspects of a cruise holiday, and one of the rare delightful moments is to simply relax on board a ship while most of the passengers are out exploring.

So what could we have done?

Well, there is always the tour of the city that is a standard offering at any port around the world. Perhaps called 'An Introduction to…' or 'Panoramic tour of…' they are perfect to show passengers around the major tourist attraction, cathedrals, monuments, and parks plus they normally give a little free time to shop.

Another popular trip on the island is the look at 'Ancient Sardinia' where visitors can spread their wings a little further from Cagliari.

For something a little more quirky, the 'Folk Dances of Sardinia' took people into the countryside to look at the cultural aspects of the local people and had the treat of some dancing as well.

A little less inspiring is the transfer from the ship to a nearby beach, in order to spend the day on the sand and check out the temperature of the water.

Many passengers will look at their port guides and tourist maps before allowing one of the local taxi drivers to whisk them to the cathedral or museums. Quite often an enterprising taxi driver will offer their services to become a tour guide for half a day and show the visitors around the city or the island. This can be very good value, but a price needs to be agreed before getting into the car.

Even on a relatively small island there is enough on offer to keep cruise ship passengers happy, although many will be like us and just enjoy the Mediterranean summer sunshine on the decks of their floating home.

+++

I have been on a cruise a couple of times when it was my birthday, and this time, Tuesday 27th July 2010, found us anchored off Sardinia with Palau just a short distance away from us. We were on the new *Arcadia* and the tenders were ready to take passengers ashore by just after 8:00 am.

As often the case we had not booked a tour, but the morning was a treat for me as we started with breakfast on our cabin balcony. Captain Ian Walters must have known about our plans and parked the ship with the glorious morning sunshine flooding in on us. Fresh orange juice, croissants and jam, Danish pastries and yoghurt as well as a pot of coffee made a delightful start to the day...and all at no extra cost.

By mid-morning we were ashore and strolling along the sea front. Once away from the town centre we saw a sandy beach next to some stunning rock formations. At one point there was a seabird sunning itself on a rock with tiny waves splashing up around it. Neither of us knew what sort of bird it was but it just seemed so proud and enjoying the attention we were giving it.

The people of Palau have done a good job making the walk along the seafront a bit special with lots of paved sections that meander among the rocks allowing nature to continue undisturbed while tourists can see the different flowers, shrubs, trees and cacti. Now and then there are small patches of grass with a monument or a statue. We saw a lot of the passengers stretching their legs and enjoying the view and even caught a glimpse of Sue Holderness (Marlene from 'Only Fools and Horses') who was having a walk before joining *Arcadia* as a celebrity guest speaker.

After an hour or so we had seen enough and were ready to make our way back again. Of course there was a chance for an ice-cream before we jumped on our tender towards the ship.

...well, Italian ice-cream is probably the best we have found anywhere in the world

Our afternoon was another chance to relax and laze in the sun, with the occasional dip in the swimming pool to cool down. Rushing around was out of the question that day and as the evening approached, the anchors rattled their way back into the hull and *Arcadia* said goodbye to Palau. We had a birthday dinner in the speciality restaurant known then as Arcadian Rhodes, and the food was deliciously superb and washed down with a glass or two of champagne.

It had been a wonderful day and very much a birthday to remember.

That was our last visit to Sardinia so far, and perhaps we have not explored it very much, but we have always enjoyed this beautiful area of the Mediterranean.

Elba

We were on our very special (old) *Arcadia* cruise in 2001, and on Saturday 28th July the ship was anchored in a sheltered bay just off the island of Elba. By 7:30 am our breakfast was over and the lifeboats-come-tenders were already in the water waiting to take passengers ashore.

So where is Elba?

Well it is a small island about 30 miles east of the French island of Corsica and perhaps seven or eight miles west of the mainland Italian port of Piombino. You may have never heard of Piombino: it sits about a third of the way between Livorno and Rome. Now when I said Elba was a small island, it is actually the third largest one under the Italian flag after Sicily and Sardinia. It is about 12 miles long from west to east and not much more than a couple of miles from north to south. It has a population of about 30,000 people, with most of them living in the capital town of Portoferraio.

The island has a lot of hills and small mountains that allow spectacular views down to the bays and coastal villages. This is important as the main industry is tourism, although many decades ago the island was a major iron ore producer.

Enough of the facts and figures.

We had a tour booked to show us around the island so we grabbed our bits as soon as breakfast was over and with tickets collected we queued for the tender. Oh by the way, it was hot again.

Once ashore in Portoferraio, our guide rounded up her party and we boarded our coach. She was a friendly guide but her accent sounded as if she came from the Philippines rather than Italy. We set off across the island and listened to her commentary, giving us a basic introduction to Elba. We learnt about its most famous inhabitant, Napoleon Bonaparte, who was exiled there in 1814. As we drove towards the more mountainous western side our guide became quite poetic with her descriptions, but the language was becoming an obstacle. At one point she was talking about the industry and having told us that the iron mines were now closed she started to tell us what the island did now, but the sentence tailed off, and we never found out. A few minutes later she asked us to look at a particular mountain and remarked that it was pretty and asked us if we thought so too.

It was just an unremarkable mountain!!!

Anyway, the coach came to a little fishing harbour called Marciana Marina where we had a few minutes to explore and buy souvenirs. The guide told us to look out for *Drunken Cake* as a speciality of the island. I am not sure if it is still the case but apparently in 2001 Elba had just one cow whose primary function was to teach the children about them. Hence there were little or no dairy products on the island and so the famous cake uses alcohol for moisture.

Yes we bought some, and it was extremely tasty.

Our stop at the harbour allowed us a chance for a relaxed stroll along the quayside and to look at the shops but it was soon time to get back on the coach to continue our tour. From Marciana we made our way back across the island. Our final stop was at the remains of a Roman Villa at a place called Punta delle Grotte. Now at this moment in my life archaeology did not sit highly on my list of interests, and this site was little more than an occasional section of knee high wall amongst a number of piles of stones. Our visit to this Roman relic came just a couple of days after visiting Pompeii and Rome, and unfortunately the archaeological remains we saw in those places were truly spectacular, so what we were seeing here paled in comparison.

There was one positive aspect to the site however. The hilltop location had a wonderful view out across Portoferraio Bay with our ship at anchor, looking absolutely beautiful.

Back on the coach we completed our drive back to the port and finished our time on Elba by looking around the shops near the harbour. Soon we jumped on a tender boat and we were back on board *Arcadia* in time for a late lunch.

Elba was a lovely island with beautiful views of mountains and coastal villages. I would certainly recommend it to people considering a visit there, but with a health warning that we hadn't seen a lot of tourist attractions back in 2001. I actually think I liked it because it was so *untouristy* and unprepared for cruise ship passengers' demands. Maybe by now the island has geared itself up to attract visitors and tempt them to open their purses and wallets, but at that time it felt different from the other places, and perhaps that is why it fascinated me.

We have never been back, and I have not seen it as a port on any cruises in the P&O brochure in more recent years, but then again I haven't been looking for it particularly, so I might have missed it. Yes I would like to go back to see it another time to explore a little deeper.

So what else did Elba offer *Arcadia*'s passengers in terms of organised tours? Well apart from our 'Tour of the Island' we could have had a more comprehensive look at the 'The Scenic Centre' or the 'East' of the island. A themed trip apparently followed 'The Footsteps of Napoleon', and there was one final offering of 'Leisurely Elba'. This was not the most varied or dynamic set of tours I have seen over the years.

Late in the afternoon we finished sun-worshipping and began to get ready for the Individual Quiz and a drink before dinner. Captain Reid made his usual announcement and retrieved the anchors to allow *Arcadia* to sail on to its next port. There was a treat on board during the evening with the Caribbean Party Night out on deck by the swimming pool. Many of the passengers wore their tropical shirts and the resident band played all the usual party songs while the entertainment team encouraged us to drink just a little more than usual. The evening ended with streamers fired up in the air from party poppers making a glorious tangle of coloured paper while we danced around the deck.

It had been a rather nice day.

North Africa - Morocco

With ports in Italy discussed, our cruise around the Mediterranean has turned towards home with the southern coast of Europe on our right (starboard side) and the North African coast on the left (port side). As yet Deb and I have never visited anywhere on this African coastline, but P&O has occasionally stopped at a couple of ports in the country of Morocco.

Morocco is the westernmost of the North African countries and lies across the water from Spain and Gibraltar. It is no more than a few miles across the Straits from the European continent. The two ports that I know have been visited are Tangiers and Casablanca. The most recent cruises I have seen comments about were to Casablanca so I will restrict my short review of the country to here.

Although not the country's capital, Casablanca is the largest city in Morocco, and is actually outside of the Mediterranean Sea, just a little way down Morocco's coast to the south. Its name means *White House* and the city has a population of around 4 million people.

There has been a lot of historical French influence, and Casablanca is probably most famous as the setting for the 1942 film of the same name starring Humphrey Bogart and Ingrid Bergman.

Passengers from ships regularly visit the King Hassan II Mosque and the bustling Souk (market).

For those of you who have concerns about visiting a mosque because of religious issues, I suggest that at least once in your life to throw away any preconceptions you may have and take a look around. Try and forget religion, and look at the beauty and magnificence of these buildings that are often as architecturally spectacular as anything in the world and decorated to unbelievable standards. Yes there are rules about footwear, and sometimes the ladies have to cover their heads and even occasionally have a full body covering, but it is worth it…I promise.

A Souk is an experience to beat your local farmers' market. In some cities there are separate ones for gold, spices, clothes, or general produce, but I believe the one in Casablanca is a general one. They are where the locals shop for their daily needs, and where tourists come to find bargains. Prices are open to negotiation, and the bravest haggler can get away with ridiculous bargains, although many of the more reserved British visitors maintain the market stallholder's profit by paying over the odds.

Cruise ship tours may take you out of Casablanca for a few miles to Rabat, which is the capital of Morocco.

As I said, I have not been there but I have looked at feedback on various forum pages and the comments have not been overly positive about Casablanca and other cruise stops in North Africa in the recent past. I must point out that people who post on these forums are often the ones who have had a bad experience, and many hundreds of people may have had wonderful experiences, so take them as a guide rather than the full truth.

I will say no more about Morocco for fear of upsetting the people of that country, or giving the wrong impression based on hearsay.

Time to go home

That completes my cruise around the Western Mediterranean Sea and it is time for me and Deb to make the homeward journey.

Leaving the Straits of Gibraltar for us isn't the end of our holidays but it is the moment when we know there are just a couple of days left. Thoughts turn to making the most of the ship, and any remaining warm sunshine, before the unpredictable British weather takes over again.

As the ship sets a course to follow the western coastline of Spain, the sea usually turns a little less gentle and its colour becomes darker. Our floating hotel is less steady as the Atlantic swell reminds us that we are on a ship that nature can toss around to test the stomachs of passengers.

The ship and especially the entertainment team continue to keep the passengers busy. There are the usual deck games, or quizzes, and sometimes there are talks with the captain, or demonstrations by the different teams on the ship. We have found out about how the toilets work, different types of rope used on the ship, how to make a bed and the magic of carving and creating displays with melons.

Hopefully the sun will be warm enough for another day on the sun-loungers around the pool, but if not the ship still has wonderful places to sit and read or dream about what holiday to have next.

In the restaurants the food will be just as good and this might be the time to splash out a cover charge to sample the fine dining venues for an extra special meal. The bars and cabaret lounges will carry on tempting us to have an extra drink or two especially on the final formal night with dinner jackets and long dresses. And of course the ship's theatre troupe will give their last performance to thrill us all.

Eventually the Bay of Biscay will dominate thoughts and yes it can be an angry 24 hours, but we have had several crossings where it is as gentle as a sleeping cat. Crossing the bay also heralds the moment when the suitcases have to be dragged out from under the bed and repacked.

...why do we always bring too many clothes?

All too soon we will be saying goodbye to dinner table mates, our waiters, and any friends we have made on the cruise. When bedtime comes it will be one of the rare nights when an alarm clock is needed to ensure we get up in time for breakfast. When we wake up again it will be in Southampton and the crew will want us off the ship as quickly as possible to prepare for the next couple of thousand eager passengers.

Hardly before breakfast has been forgotten we will be off the ship and finding our luggage before loading it into the car again. That drive home is always sad and we don't say very much to each other.

Back home a cup of tea is the first priority, before the suitcases are emptied, and washing started. Unused clothes and bits are returned to drawers and wardrobes as quickly as possible. The reason to get things out of the way quickly is that we know we will soon start to suffer from a strange sensation of what we call *Land Sickness*. It's very similar to the early stages of sea-sickness and is a result of our bodies getting used to not feeling the ship's movement anymore.

In the evening it is time to relax on our larger and more comfortable chairs or settees and catch up with the first of television programmes recorded while we have been away. But it won't be long before our thoughts turn to when we can have another cruise.

Cruising has opened up so many opportunities to see places around the world that I never thought I would visit. My only regret is that it took so many years to discover the magic.

"So Deb where do you fancy going next?"

About the Author

George Williams was born and brought up in and around the town of Helston in Cornwall.

His working life was in the Telecommunications industry, starting as an engineer but finally moving into training. The job eventually forced him to move with his wife Deb and their two children from his beloved Cornwall. After a short period in Oxfordshire they moved again and settled in Staffordshire.

The author has a severe phobia of flying, so to celebrate the couple's silver wedding anniversary in 2000 they took a *one-off* holiday of a lifetime on a cruise around the Mediterranean.

George and Deb fell in love with cruising and it became their first choice of holiday every year after that time. In 2012 they had their most exciting cruise with a circumnavigation of the world lasting more than three months.

The author is now retired and one of his hobbies is writing, especially about the cruises that he and his wife have enjoyed.

Other books by this author

A Cornishman Goes Cruising

A Cornishman Cruises to Venice

Around the World without Wings

Time for Tea and a Cheese Scone

Would You Like Some Plums?

Printed in Great Britain
by Amazon